Become a Compassionate CareGiver

Reduce Stress. Avoid Burnout.

Richard Anastasi

Copyright © 2016 by Richard Anastasi

All rights reserved. This book or any portion thereof
may not be reproduced or used in any manner whatsoever
without the express written permission of the publisher
except for the use of brief quotations in a book review.

Printed in the United States of America

First Printing, 2016

ISBN-13 978-0-692-70152-2
ISBN-10 0-692-70152-4

rjanastasi@gmail.com
http://caregiverja.com

I dedicate this book to those
who first taught me about care giving:

**My sister, Gloria Anastasi,
Who always cared for me.**
(cancer – adeno carcinoma)
(November 29, 1948 – August 7, 1981)

**My father, Alfred Anastasi,
Who showed me how much he cared.**
(heart disease)
(August 24, 1918 – March 15, 1994)

**My mother, Mary Anastasi,
Who taught me how to care.**
(liver disease – primary biliary cirrhosis)
(May 3, 1921 – March 14, 2004)

Prologue And I Closed the Book	5
Introduction	9
Chapter 1 Lead Us Not Into [the] Temptation…of Doing	21
Chapter 2 It's In How You Approach the Task: The Origin of the P-Dance	27
Chapter 3 Becoming a Compassionate Presence	31
Chapter 4 "But I Gotta Do Something"…Yes, Listen	39
Chapter 5 Starting With the End in Mind	45
Chapter 6 The Healing Power of Place	51
Chapter 7 Stop Fixin' the Disease – Heal the Person	57
Chapter 8 Pain & Suffering	63
Chapter 9 Grief & Loss	71
Chapter 10 Make Memories, Not Misery	77
Chapter 11 "When the Music's Over…Turn Out the Lights"	85
Wrapping Up	91
Epilogue	93
Acknowledgments	95
Notes	99
Resources	105
Bibliography	111

Prologue   And I Closed the Book

I closed the book, placed it on the table, and finally, decided to walk out the door. The book was one of a two volume set[1] which gave me comfort while caring for my mother. She was living with the pain caused by the effects of a liver that was dying. About ten years earlier, a biopsy confirmed that she had primary biliary cirrhosis[2], a liver disease with no known cure other than a transplant.

I reached for the doorknob. Looking back, my eyes fell once again on my mother, Mary. She was in a coma, lying on the bed in her room at the hospice facility. Her chest barely rose as she struggled for her next breath. I heard the air caught at the back of her throat as it rattled the substances stuck there. There, on her back, eyes closed, at peace, is the scene I captured of her as I was getting ready to leave.

I was feeling guilty that I could not bear to spend another moment in that room waiting for my mother to die. It was all that I could do to sit there and read, and sometimes to pray. It was hard being there, being there with nothing left to do for her, nothing left to say.

I wanted to be there for her as she had been there for me. So many times, as a child, mommy wiped the dirt, the hurt, or the tears from my cheeks, sometimes with a damp wash cloth, and sometimes with spit and a tissue. Why couldn't I stay with her for one more hour, one more minute? I had nowhere to go -- no wife, no children to care for. When I left, I would be leaving to go to an empty apartment – her apartment.

It once was our apartment. It was where we all used to live together, we, as in my father, my mother, me, and my older sister, Gloria. Now it was her apartment. She lived there by herself. Gloria died before her 33rd birthday on August 7, 1981. The 10th anniversary of my father's death, March 15, 1994, was coming up in two days.

To care for my mother, I had moved back to New York City where I grew up. I was now living in the same bedroom in her apartment where I had spent most of my adolescence and some of my adulthood until I had moved out for good.

No, I didn't want to go back to her apartment tonight – at least not right away. Tonight was not a night for me to be alone with my thoughts.

Then, I noticed the book on the table. For a year, that book and its companion had accompanied me on my journey of care giving. I started to go back for it but remembered I had already finished reading it just a few minutes ago. No sense taking it with me now.

I couldn't remain in the hospice room any longer. Quietly, I closed the door.

Little did I know that that was the last time I would see my mother alive.

I walked down the carpeted hallway of the hospice facility towards the elevators. The walls of this hospice facility were painted in pastel colors of green, blue, and pink. I boarded an elevator and made my way quickly through the lobby.

My next thought was where to go for dinner. Should I walk down First Avenue to Simone's or take the bus home and make dinner? Even if the friendly bartender wasn't there, it would do me good to eat surrounded by the conversation of others.

I began walking down First Avenue towards Simone's.

It was getting dark by the time I reached Simone's. There weren't many diners or people at the bar. Pulling up a bar stool, I asked the bar tender for a menu, and (I really don't remember now) ordered a Stella Artois on tap, my drink of choice at that time.

I didn't stay long after eating dinner. The conversations around me brought me no comfort.

My next decision was whether to take the Second Avenue bus home or walk. On weekends, the buses don't run as regularly as they do during the week. I figured that by the time I waited for the bus to arrive, I could be a third of the way home. I began walking.

I had walked home many times over the past 10 months since that fateful day on the platform of the Long Island Railroad waiting for the train back to Manhattan.

Early in 2003, I had started working for a small California based software company. A member of the board of directors had recommended me to this company. He had hoped that with my prior experience, I could help turn around the fortunes of his company. It was a good fit.

As VP of Field Operations, I traveled nationally from my home in Irving, Texas to visit customers, sales prospects, and software distribution partners. I was making multiple trips to New York City to develop relationships with our larger clients and software distribution partners. These trips gave me an opportunity to visit with my mother. When I came to New York, I stayed with her. I rationalized that it was saving the company money on hotels.

One week, I was once again in New York. The chair of the board and his CEO had also come to New York to meet with our software distributor on Long Island to discuss our distribution agreement.

There was irony in this visit. I used to work for this distribution partner. It was this same software company that transferred me to Texas in April of 1989. It was the reason I was no longer living close to my mother. Now, 14 years later, I was leaving their corporate headquarters with the senior managers of the software company I had joined in January.

The purpose of the meeting was to strengthen our distribution channel. I didn't think the meeting went well. Waiting for our train on the platform of a Long Island Railroad station for our return trip back to Manhattan, it was quiet. No one was talking. Each of us seemed to be lost in thought. It was a beautiful spring day in the third week of May.

Then, the chair of the board came up to me and said: "Richard, you know it's going to take a 110% of your effort to help us turn this company around. And I know that you are trying to care for your mother. You can't do both. If you decide to leave, we'll pay you until the end of the month."

Many emotions hit me at once. Shock – can I afford to be without a job now? Disappointment – I had hoped there would be a way to continue working while caring for my mother. Anger – Why wasn't there another way? Fear – Can I care for my mother if I don't have a job?

All I knew for sure was that I was going to care for my mother. I would no longer be working for this company.

I don't remember exactly what I said. With this storm of emotions stirring within, somehow, I managed to stay calm. I made some reply indicating that my choice was to care for my mother.

That was how I began the life of a CareGiver™.

Introduction

"We don't think ourselves into a new way of living; we live ourselves into a new way of thinking."
                    The Eighth Core Principle of the Center for Action and Contemplation.
                                                            Richard Rohr, O.F.M.

I am writing this book to share with you, dear CareGiver™, what I have learned thus far about becoming a compassionate CareGiver. My education began in earnest when I returned home to New York City at the end of May in 2003 to care for my mother, Mary Anastasi. I was with her as she dealt with the symptoms of liver disease. She died less than two months before her 83rd birthday on March 14, 2004.

The wisdom I gained about care giving comes from three sources: from reflecting on my own experiences as a CareGiver; from the conversations I had with my mother, other CareGivers, and professionals who deal with end-of-life issues; and from the research I did about care giving, about living well, and about dying well.

Most of us begin as CareGivers when we get the news that a loved one has a terminal disease. The news catches us off-guard. It shocks us. When we get over the stun of the shocking news, we typically launch into mobilization. We want to do whatever we can to fight the disease. Too often, this focus on mobilization leads us on a downward spiral which ends in burnout. My intent is that by reading this book, you will not only avoid burnout, but you will also be able to reduce the stress that comes with being a CareGiver.

Gail Sheehy, a New York Times bestselling author, documents this downward spiral in her 2010 book, **Passages in Caregiving**[1]. In it she describes how she cared for her husband, Clay Felker, founder of *New York* magazine. For the last 17 years of his life, she cared for him as he dealt with three bouts of throat cancer. Sheehy documents well the progression in care giving from what she calls "shock and mobilization" to the point of burnout. When a CareGiver feels like and says, "I can't do this anymore!" the CareGiver has reached the point of burnout.

Sheehy relates how she reached burnout. She describes what lead her to feel as though she could no longer go on caring for her husband. She recovered and went on to care for him. Together, they reached the final stage she calls "the long goodbye."

The purpose of **this** book is to provide insights into how you can become a compassionate CareGiver without spiraling down to that place where you feel like saying "I can't do this anymore!" My hope is that by applying what you learn in this book, you will avoid burnout. More importantly, you'll learn an attitude of service that will be of benefit to you, dear CareGiver, and the person you are caring for, the CaredFor.

Throughout this book, I intentionally spell the word *CareGiver*™ as one word beginning with a capital C and with a capital G beginning the word Giver. I do this to denote a person who is adopting the new paradigm for care giving which I am proposing.

I refer to the person the CareGiver is caring for as 'the CaredFor.'

You are reading this book because you are a CareGiver, or you expect to become a CareGiver, or maybe because you know someone who is or has been a CareGiver. You are seeking 'food for the journey' of care giving. Caregiving is indeed a journey. As with other journeys, care giving is more about the journey than the destination.

I have written this book from the perspective of someone who has already been through the journey of care giving. My perspective is to be your CareGiver Guide.

I begin by telling you about three opportunities I had to become a CareGiver. With each opportunity, I responded differently. Each opportunity taught me important lessons. Your path to becoming a CareGiver will be different, but I expect you will gain insight from the ways I responded.

1. **Care giving for my sister – or not.**

My first opportunity to become a CareGiver occurred in January of 1981 when an oncologist had taken my parents and me aside to tell us that my sister, Gloria, had six months to live. We were in the corridor outside of

Gloria's room in Mother Cabrini Hospital in New York City. The oncologist told us that Gloria had adeno carcinoma. Adeno carcinoma is a form of cancer that affects the body's soft tissues.

My parents and I cried. It was fair to say we were in a state of shock. The news was too hard for us to take in all at once.

I saw first-hand how my mother and father took on the role of care givers as Gloria succumbed to this form of cancer.

My father told his boss what was going on. Through his influence, my father got Gloria admitted to one of the top cancer research hospitals in Manhattan.

My mother quit her job to be available to care for my sister. In the last weeks of Gloria's life, my mother was there at her side every day and many nights, too.

My mother acted as if a cure might be around the corner. She felt if only we could keep Gloria alive long enough, she could be to beneficiary of a newly discovered cure. I prayed for a cure, but I don't think I really believed it would happen.

Consciously or not, I had distanced myself from being involved in caring for my sister. I was in denial about her imminent death. Though my sister and I were close growing up, I had a difficult time being with her knowing she had less than a year to live. I didn't know what to say to her about her having cancer. I didn't know what to do. I left that to the doctors, the nurses, and mostly to my mother.

At first, the chemotherapy was working. For a while, Gloria held on to her job at Peat Marwick where she was a senior course developer in their corporate training department. The chemotherapy led to the loss of her naturally rich black hair. Her hair loss made her reluctant to continue her social life outside of work.

Her friends convinced her to get a wig. With her wig, Gloria felt more comfortable both at work and when out with her friends. Unfortunately, after a few months, she didn't have the energy to do her job well.

While she had to quit her job, she continued to live independently in her studio apartment in the Chelsea area of Manhattan. Her studio was on the 4th floor of a walk-up building.

Eventually, the daily climb of the four flights of steps became too much for her to manage. My mother encouraged her to move back home to our apartment. Her bedroom was still as it was when she moved out several years before.

In the same month that Gloria started complaining about a pain on the right side of her back, the first clue that something was wrong, I had started a new job at a major systems software company, Applied Data Research. The job involved travel. This gave me a reason for not being around to care for her. As she went in and out of hospitals for treatment, I would dutifully visit her with my parents. Yet, I don't recall ever visiting Gloria on my own.

It wasn't like she had been hospitalized in another state hundreds of miles away or that I didn't have an easy way to get to the hospital. The hospitals were all in Manhattan where there is convenient public transportation and plenty of taxis. On top of that, I had my own car which I used daily to get to work. I didn't have an excuse that it was hard to go see her.

By August of 1981, it was clear the end was approaching. She had now survived 10 months, 4 months longer than the original prognosis. Gloria died three months short of her 33rd birthday on August 7, 1981.

What caused this strange form of cancer? No one would say. Unlike other cancers, it didn't lodge in a specific organ. It wasn't breast cancer, lung cancer, or pancreatic cancer. Adeno carcinoma is a cancer which grows in the body's soft tissues.

It showed up first as fluids outside her right lung and spread from there. Little tumors were all over her body. She had lost a lot of weight, but her mind was sharp. As her pain increased, her oncologist increased the level of pain killers. Gloria maintained a level of awareness despite the increase in the pain medication.

I remember her asking to see me three days before she died. I came to see her early that Tuesday morning before going off to work. I think at that point she knew her death was near. She wanted to make sure she could say good-bye to her baby brother.

I came into her room. I stood at the foot of her bed. She was barely conscious, fighting off the effects of the pain killers so she could make some contact with me. I said something to her; I don't remember what and left. I didn't even go over to kiss her goodbye. I just left.

The day she died, I was at work in the Paramus, New Jersey office of the software company I had recently joined. It was a Friday afternoon. My father called me at the office. He said, "my Little Pigeon is gone." It was a term of endearment he had for her.

My mother later told me at that around 3 o'clock, Gloria turned over on her side, and died. She knew the hospital routine. Nothing happens on weekends. The primary care physicians leave for their weekends away. The staff that remains provides little more than maintenance care. By this point, Gloria had had enough. Rather than spend one more weekend in the hospital, she decided to leave.

So, ended my first experience of participating or rather not participating, in the care of someone I loved dearly. With my sister, I would characterize my care giving as one of denial. I did as little as possible. Not exactly what you would expect from someone who claimed he had a special bond with his sister.

I was in denial about Gloria's dying while she was alive, and I was in denial about grieving for her after she died. Rather than giving myself an opportunity to grieve, I returned to establishing myself in my new job.

I saw the impact Gloria's death had on my mother. She barely talked to my father and me for almost a year. She began sleeping in Gloria's bedroom and remained there for most of the day. She would prepare meals and maintain the household as she had done before, but she kept to herself. My mother lost not only her daughter but her best friend. That dual loss was overwhelming.

She was angry about the care Gloria received during the last weeks of her life. My mother was at her side all of the time. From her perspective, the treatment killed her daughter. From what she saw, the doctors and staff were doing nothing to keep her alive. They were just waiting for her to die. From her point of view, they may have even worked to bring her life to an end sooner than later by increasing the pain medication and feeding her nothing but a 'thin soup.'

Sorrow and anger dominated her life the year after Gloria died.

I could do little to relieve my mother's sorrow. I listened to her anger over Gloria's treatment. I didn't try to dissuade her from writing to the hospital administrator complaining about the way they treated Gloria. The hospital administrator responded with a two-page page letter addressing her issues. She didn't agree with the response. She didn't answer back.

For my part, I was not sensitive to my own feelings. As I said, I focused on work. The guilt and regret I felt about not participating in caring for my sister stayed suppressed. In my mind, I had failed my sister. I didn't want to think about or feel what that meant to me.

It was that suppressed guilt and regret over how little care I gave Gloria that resulted in a flood of tears one night, six years after her death. I cried for almost 30 minutes driving home one night after work. I had finally allowed myself to grieve.

What did this first opportunity to be a CareGiver teach me? Looking back through the lens of experience, I learned I could have made it easier on myself had I been able to tell Gloria what I was feeling. Before she got cancer, I could talk to her about what was on my mind. Usually she sensed something was wrong and approached me first. Why didn't I trust that we could still talk to each other openly and honestly? I had let the fears and discomfort I had about dying, and death come between us.

2. Caregiving for my father – being absent.

Life presents us with the same issue again and again until we learn to face that issue well. I had a second opportunity to be a CareGiver when my father's heart disease finally caught up with him in the winter of 1994. While he never had had a heart attack or stroke, he suffered from persistent angina pain for the last 20 years of his life.

In January of 1976, he had his first triple heart-bypass surgery. The surgery was technically successful: the surgeons grafted new coronary arteries to improve the flow of blood to his heart. Unfortunately, the surgery didn't provide the relief his cardiologists expected. He had another triple heart-bypass surgery in July.

Again, the surgery was technically successful, but it did not fully relieve his angina pain. He survived the next 19 years on blood thinners and nitro glycerin pills. He would slip a nitro pill under his tongue when the pain was acute.

In 1994, even the nitro pills didn't provide relief. He and his doctors had to decide whether to risk another bypass surgery. I was told by a friend that the survival rate of a third bypass surgery was 5%. Nonetheless, that was the route my father chose. In getting ready for the surgery, he asked my mother if she would arrange for me to fly home to visit with him.

Again, I was at a transition in my career. A few months earlier, I started working as an independent IT (information technology) consultant for a start-up software company. The president of that company was responsible for my transfer to Irving, TX in 1989. I was still living there.

After talking it over with my mother, we decided there was nothing much I could do for my father at this point. I thought it was more important to attend to my new career. I would come back to New York after the surgery.

He died on the operating table. I never got the chance to say goodbye in person - another care giving opportunity with less than a desirable outcome. A lesson learned here was not to take for granted that there will be time to be supportive of someone you care for.

There was one more opportunity to become a CareGiver. I told most of that story in the Prologue.

3. Caregiving for my mother – on the job training.

About ten years before my father died, my mother found out she had primary biliary cirrhosis. The doctors told her there was nothing they could do at that point except to continue to monitor her liver. As I later learned, it usually takes 10 to 15 years after the diagnosis before the symptoms of primary biliary cirrhosis begin to show up. In March of 2003, the symptoms of that disease began to manifest.

As I wrote in the Prologue, I was now working for a struggling storage software company. Two months earlier, at the suggestion of a member of their board of directors, whom I had met at an alumni fund-raising dinner, I accepted the position as VP of Field Operations. The board member expected that I could help turn the company around given my background in storage software sales and support.

By April of that year, the symptoms of the liver disease caused my mother more pain. Her personal physician told us that her best option was a liver transplant. We met with the head of the kidney and liver transplant service at a large hospital complex in New York City. He scheduled some tests.

When we returned the following week to hear the test results, he told us that he could not put her on the liver transplant list. Even if there were a liver available, he said, it was unlikely she could survive the transplant operation at her age. That decision was effectively a death sentence. The liver would only get worse.

As VP of Field Operations, I had the flexibility to travel anywhere in the country. This made it possible to continue to visit my mother. I rationalized the increase in the number of trips to New York as part of my approach to improve our relationships with one of the company's largest customers and its biggest distributor. Both had operations in New York. Besides, the company was saving on the cost of hotels and meals by my staying with my mother.

At the end May of 2003, the chair of the board of our software company and the CEO invited me to go along with them to a meeting with our largest software distributor at its corporate headquarters on Long Island.

In the Prologue, I described what happened after that meeting. As I wrote, while standing on the platform of the Long Island Railroad for our return trip to Manhattan, the chair of the board took me aside. As I recall, this is what he said to me. "Richard, I am going to need 110% of your effort to help turn this company around. And I know you are trying to care for your mother. You can't do both. If you decide to leave, I will pay you until the end of the month."

I heard these words with shock and disbelief. But the chairman's words were clear. I had to make a choice: stay and work to turn the company around or care for my mother. From his point of view, I couldn't do both. As he said, if I chose to leave, he would pay me to the end of May, barely two weeks away.

How could I turn my back on my mother? The chair of the board had made it clear I couldn't be involved in the care of my mother and remain working there. I didn't think his decision was fair. I thought there was a way I could do both.

In retrospect, it was good he presented me with a clear choice. Though, at the time, I didn't feel that it was good at all. I was fortunate I was in the position to make this choice. I didn't have to be concerned about the impact on a wife or children. I had neither a wife nor children. Many CareGivers do have to take into consideration the impact on their families.

Having made that choice freed me to be a CareGiver for my mother in whatever way I saw fit. I didn't have to make any compromises in caring for her. My care would no longer be dependent on figuring out how to justify a business trip to New York City. Now I would be living there. As a friend put it, "I was all in."

So, began my third opportunity to become a CareGiver.

Though "I was all in," unfortunately, I didn't know where to begin. Other than packing up clothes and moving back to my old bedroom in my mother's apartment on the lower, lower east side of Manhattan, I really didn't have a clue where to start.

The first thing someone told me to do was to have my mother apply for Medicare or was it Medicaid? Whatever it was, I was told I needed to move most of her assets out of her name or she wouldn't qualify for benefits. I had to do so as quickly as possible because of the so-called 'look back' period. The government could look back 3 years to see if any qualifying assets had been moved in an attempt to qualify. If so, they would still be counted in determining her eligibility.

I was also told I needed to get a power of attorney on her behalf; file a medical directive with the hospital at which she had been receiving treatment; set up a living will, and on and on.

It was all about do this, do that, do, do, do.

I went on the Internet and found a lawyer who offered to do all that for one fee -- $4,000. He also highly recommended I hire an elder care consultant to help me through the process of applying for Medicaid and to advise me on other care needs.

Being a good doer, I did as I was told. I paid the $4,000 for a package of legal documents a half-inch thick. I hired the elder care consultant at $125 per hour.

At that time, those seemed like good choices. I have learned since then that I could have achieved the same results for a lot less money. There are free resources on the web which you can use to generate customized documents that will meet the basic requirements of a family CareGiver. These resources are a place to start. As each situation is different and often more complex than the situation I had with my mother, I recommend consulting a qualified elder care lawyer to review any documents you generate with automated tools.

As for the elder care consultant, after a few weeks of her services, I dismissed her. My mother had a life-threatening illness with a prognosis of less than a year. It wasn't possible to make any adjustments to her assets because it would fall within the 'look back' period. In my situation, I didn't see the need for an elder care consultant.

Again, your situation will be different from mine. You may indeed find value in hiring a qualified consultant. Search under the term "geriatric care manager." There are organizations that offer certifications for becoming a geriatric care manager, though as far as I am aware, there is no legal requirement to pass a certification course before using the title of 'geriatric care manager.' Be sure to get references before engaging elder care consultants, regardless of their titles or certifications.

At first, I felt good about all this. I was getting into action. I appeared to have a plan. Everything would work out.

As the saying goes, "When man plans, God laughs."

Despite my appearance of having a plan, I still really didn't know what I was doing.

I looked for a book or two that might help clarify what I should be doing. A friend, I wish I could remember who it was, suggested I read Dr. Rachel Remen's **Kitchen Table Wisdom**[2]. At the time, that book was sold in a set with a companion book, My **Grandfather's Blessings**[3]. These weren't exactly the "how to do caring giving" books I was looking for, but they were a source of comfort, nonetheless.

Kitchen Table Wisdom shares the author's insights gathered from her medical practice and working with those treating the terminally ill.

The other book, **My Grandfather's Blessings,** tells of the wisdom her grandfather, an orthodox Jewish rabbi, instilled in her while he looked after her when she came home from school. Both her parents were doctors and couldn't be there when she returned from school. She was about 5 years old. She reflected on that wisdom as an adult as she continued her medical practice.

These two books were my constant companions during my caregiving experience with my mother. While they didn't teach me what to do, they assisted me in developing a 'way of being' with my mother.

I read the last page of one of the two books in this set (I don't remember which book) in my mother's hospice room the Saturday afternoon before she died. She died less than 8 hours later at around 2 a.m. Sunday morning.

As I said, the books never told me what to do. They did provide solace during the months I spent with my mother. They gave me perspective on how to *be* a CareGiver.

I hope, dear CareGiver, that this book at least does that for you – becomes a source of solace. My greatest hope for you is that this book teaches you not so much what to do but how to be, how to **be**come a CareGiver, a compassionate presence in the life of another. By doing so, I believe you will be able to reduce the stress of being a CareGiver and avoid burnout.

Chapter 1   Lead Us Not Into [the] Temptation…of Doing

The focus of the existing paradigm of care giving is *doing*. "What do I **do** now?" It is the first question a care giver asks after getting the news that someone they care about has a terminal illness. Until we shift the paradigm of care giving away from a primary focus on *doing* to one of *being*, care giving will continue to be about struggle, effort, frustration and, burnout.

Before we can shift a paradigm, it would help to define what I mean by a paradigm. A paradigm is a set of habits, beliefs, and ways of thinking learned from parents, teachers, coaches, friends, and other significant people in our lives, and from our culture. We acquire most of what makes up our paradigm by the age of 3.

As we grow older, the paradigm becomes embedded in our unconscious mind as a set of limiting and unexamined beliefs. Our paradigm affects our actions and reactions. Our paradigm is embedded in our intentions, in what we give our attention to, and, in our actions. Within a paradigm of doing, there is little or no room for a concern with the way we are being.

The current paradigm of care giving focuses on fixing problems. If there is a problem, let's **do** something about it. Let's fix it. Care giving works on fixing three problems: death, the disease, and the one dying. Yes, the person with the disease gets turned into a problem to fix.

Why bother shifting the paradigm of care giving? "To ignore the power of paradigms to influence your judgment is to put yourself at risk when exploring the future." [1] Shifting the paradigm of care giving from doing to being will reduce the stress in the life of a CareGiver. We'll examine this premise as we discuss the three problems created by the paradigm of doing: death, the disease, and the one dying.

The Problem of Death

Care givers live in a world that treats "death as a problem to fix." Death is not a problem to fix. It is a part of life. If we realize death is not a problem, then there is nothing to fix.

Yet, until we can look death in the face and laugh, it remains our silent partner in every act and every decision we make. Dealing honestly and openly with death is the first challenge for both the CareGiver and the CaredFor. Having a relationship with death that breaks the bonds of our habitual way of thinking about it is a big first step to reduce stress in the life of a CareGiver.

Is birth a problem to fix? Birth and death are both parts of life. Yet we celebrate one and mourn the other.

At birth, we began a journey of physical growth. As we age, if we are self-aware, we learn to let go of the attachment to physical growth and the needs and wants of the ego. We enter a stage of our journey marked by diminution.[2] At this stage we start to lessen our attachments to the physical world and the demands of the ego. The ego, in its attempt to protect us, drives us to acquire possessions in the false belief that having many possessions will increase our power and then provide security.

How do we break the hold of our ego drive? By learning to let go of possessions, of relationships, especially those that no longer serve us, and to let go of even the sense of who we think we are, our ego identity.

Having possessions in and of itself is not a problem. The problem comes when we start to believe that we cannot be happy, we will not have status, we cannot be secure or in control unless we have certain possessions. In short, we become attached to having possessions because our paradigm of doing tells us they are necessary to be happy, to be esteemed, and to be secure. We come to believe our power comes from having these possessions.

The attachment to possessions then leads us to want to protect and preserve what we have accumulated. And our most prized possession is life. In this paradigm, death is the enemy of life. So, we fight death.

The issue is not living versus dying. We all live. We all die. The issue is living well[3] every time we draw a breath. Do that, and death will be nothing more to you than a sunset at the end of a day. Each sunrise will be like a new birth filled with hope and expectation of what is yet to be.

For many CareGivers, each sunrise brings up the dread of what more they will have to **do** that day. They fear what sufferings may show up. Will the CaredFor once again resist taking her pills which are now hard to swallow? Will it be hard to watch the CaredFor endure one more dialysis treatment? Will it be another day of exhaustion after a night of sleep interrupted by calls from the CaredFor?

I cared for my mother while she was struggling with the symptoms of primary biliary cirrhosis. The struggle lasted for ten months. As she struggled with the disease, I struggled with becoming a CareGiver. It was a stressful time for both of us.

The stress lessened when I stopped fighting against death.

The Problem of the Disease

As with the false problem of death, the disease itself is "not a problem to fix." A disease is the manifestation of a body which has lost its ability to heal. The problem to fix is what is in the way of the body's ability to heal. Remove the impediments that keep the body from healing, and it will heal itself. In other words, focus on maintaining the healing power of the body, not on fixing the symptoms the body is manifesting.

The disease becomes "a problem to fix" in the sense that the medical profession tends to address the effects or symptoms of the disease rather than looking at the fundamental reason why the disease is manifesting in the body in the first place.

What is interfering with the body's ability to heal? As my doctor repeatedly reminds me, "God didn't leave anything out of the body that's necessary for healing." Maximize the body's ability to heal, and the likelihood of any disease taking hold will be minimized.

This is a bold approach to health care – working on maintaining the body's ability to heal rather than prescribing medications to handle symptoms or performing surgery to remove what is damaged. If you are skeptical about this approach to health care, I strongly suggest you read **The Cancer Killers**[4].

This book tells the story of how Dr. Charlie Majors recovered from stage four bone marrow cancer without chemotherapy, radiation, or surgery. The term 'cancer killers' refers to all of us. When we have healthy immune systems, we are continually killing cancer cells. Right now, as you read this book, if your immune system is healthy, you are killing cancer cells.

We 'get cancer' when something gets in the way of our immune system's ability to kill cancer cells faster than the cancer cells are multiplying.

Dr. Majors describes the mindset he adopted to allow the body to heal. Yes, there were many things to do, but his way of being, his mindset made the difference. His mindset was: "I am a cancer killer. I will prevail!" He then worked to make that true.

Dr. Majors no longer has a brain cavity filled with malignant tumors. He and his healing team figured out what was preventing his body from healing (a high level of toxicity) and then built up his immune system so that once again it can kill cancer cells faster than cancer cells could multiply.

Address the cause, not the symptoms. Eliminate what is blocking the body's ability to heal, and then the body can begin healing itself.

Once you move beyond addressing the symptoms, once you have adopted the right mindset, you have set up the conditions to reduce the stress of managing the disease for both the CaredFor, the person with the disease, as well as for the CareGiver.

When you fight the symptoms of cancer, there is an underlying stress that comes from not knowing whether you 'got it all'. Did the surgeon cut out enough of the organ? Did the radiation burn out all the cancer cells? Did the chemotherapy kill all the cancer cells? With this approach, you just don't know. The cancer may be in remission now, but for how long?

You may ask yourself: "The colon cancer is under check, but has it spread to the kidneys?"

When you work to strengthen the immune system so that it can function well, it doesn't matter where the cancer cells are. The immune system will kill them wherever they pop up. The cancer won't recur because the immune system once again is winning the real war on cancer.

You can deal with other diseases the same way. Work to find the cause of the disease, rather than focusing on just treating symptoms. Yes, you have to deal with the symptoms while you are restoring the ability of the body to heal. But never lose focus on building up the healing power of the body and mind.

The Problem of the One Dying, the CaredFor

As CareGivers, we see the CaredFor through the lens of the disease. It shapes our relationship with the CaredFor. We do not separate our dealing with the disease from the way we relate to the CaredFor. The CareGiver tends to relate to the CaredFor the same way the CareGiver relates to the disease-- as a problem to fix. At times, they become one and the same -- both are problems to fix.

Even the CaredFor becomes identified with the disease. Patients will say "I am a diabetic," rather than saying "I have diabetes."

Medical professionals talk about obese people. A person is not obese. When you use the forms of the verb 'to be,' such as 'am' or 'is,' you are saying what goes before the verb equals what comes after it.

For example, when you say, 'I am obese' or someone tells you that you are obese, it is saying you are the disease called obesity. That's not true. Your body has a condition called 'obesity.' You are not obese. Obesity is a condition of the body. The CaredFor is not obese. The CaredFor is manifesting the symptoms of a condition called obesity.

Care giving becomes less stressful when you develop a relationship with the CaredFor as a person rather than as a disease, and not as a problem to fix. With this approach, you don't have to worry about how to treat the disease or anything about the disease. What you 'have to know' is how to relate to the CaredFor. That's what the CaredFor is looking for – someone who can relate to him the way he is now.

When I was caring for my mother, a part of me kept hoping she could be the way she was before she became ill. That only if she could have had the transplant…That only if there was an alternative treatment that could reverse the liver disease… All these thoughts kept me from being present to my mother the way she was. And that's what she wanted.

She wanted to know I was there for her no matter what. She wanted to know I would be there to care of her when she was beyond caring for herself. It didn't matter to her what I was doing or not doing day-to-day. It was my presence that gave her comfort.

Had I internalized that understanding when I began to care for my mother, I wouldn't have stressed so much about what I was doing. I was stressed wondering:
"What are the right things to be doing?"
"Am I doing enough of them?"
"What am I not doing that I should be doing?"

Once again, the paradigm of doing was raising its ugly head. That's why I keep preaching the paradigm of being. As my mother taught me, it was more important how I was being there for her than any of the individual tasks I did for her.

Throughout this book, we will learn ways to shift the way we approach death, disease, and the CaredFor and how to reduce the stress that comes from the paradigm of 'doing' CareGiving.

Chapter 2   It's In How You Approach the Task: The Origin of the P-Dance

"Well the first days are the hardest days, don't you worry any more. 'Cause when life looks like Easy Street, there is danger at your door. Think this through with me, let me know your mind, Wo, oh, what I want to know, is are you kind?"
"Uncle John's Band"
The Grateful Dead

There is a lot of truth in the lines of this song, "Uncle John's Band" by The Grateful Dead. I found that the first days of being the CareGiver for my mother were indeed the hardest because I didn't know what to do.

Figuring out what to do is the continual challenge for a new CareGiver. When you begin the life of a CareGiver, no one hands you a manual and says, "Here, read this. If you have any questions, call me." First, there's no one waiting around to hand you anything, let alone a manual on CareGiving.

Second, though a lot has been written about what to do and how to do the tasks of CareGiving, each opportunity to be a CareGiver is unique.

The person you are caring for is unique. The way the disease is progressing is unique. You, the CareGiver, are unique. The combination of these three things creates a unique situation. Yes, you can read about guidelines of how to approach care giving. There are professionals who will make recommendations for specific tasks to be performed. You will hear many suggestions about what to do. All of them can be helpful. Yet none of them can tell you what to do in every situation.

More important than knowing what to do is learning how to *be* a CareGiver. What I have learned about becoming a compassionate CareGiver is that you start with the question that ends the first stanza of "Uncle John's Band:" **Are you kind?**

Start with being kind to yourself. I say it and remind myself repeatedly: "You can't care for another unless you take care of yourself...first!"

If you can be kind to yourself, you have a chance at being kind to the person you are caring for, the CaredFor. You can't extend kindness to the CaredFor if you don't know how to be kind to yourself.

We'll talk more about how to develop being kind and compassionate later. For now, I want to get back to the 'first days are the hardest days.' The first days are hard because you are beginning a relationship with the CaredFor. The relationship you had with the CaredFor before the disease entered the picture is going to change.

Before the CaredFor contracted the disease, there was no need for her to rely on another – you, the CareGiver. The CaredFor maintained an independent life. The loss of independence and the need to rely on another fundamentally shifts the relationship between the CaredFor and the CareGiver. That's not necessarily a bad thing. It can be an opportunity to reconnect and deepen a relationship.

Here's an example of how the relationship with my mother shifted as she came to rely more on me.

In the first week or so of being with my mother, she could get around on her own. Sometimes, though, she was a little unsteady on her feet. This was particularly true after she had been sitting for a while in her favorite armchair. When she got up to go to the bathroom, her first few steps were wobbly.

To help her to steady herself, I would take hold of her hands as she began to walk. Continuing to hold her hands, I walked backwards down the corridor from the living room toward the bathroom. Once she got to the bathroom, she could get around on her own.

When she was ready, she'd let me know. After she opened the bathroom door, I reached out to hold her hands again, and then lifted her arms out in front of her for balance. I resumed walking backwards, as before, and slowly we'd arrive back to the armchair in the living room.

After a few days of doing this, it occurred to me that someone watching us might think we were dancing. I mentioned that to my mother. She smiled.

When I was younger, she danced with me when we attended the weddings of friends or members of the extended family. She was a good dancer. I enjoyed watching her dance with my father.

Remembering when we danced together, I began walking to a dance step as we walked back and forth to and from the bathroom. It was something like a cha-cha. Our walks to the bathroom were turning into dancing.

I know my mother got a kick out of this. I decided to give our little dance a name. I called it the P-Dance. The P was short for 'pee' since we were dancing because she had to 'go pee.' This is the origin of the P-Dance. Other than being a cute story, at least in my opinion, why am I writing about it?

Finding humor in the daily routine of care giving, which is boring at times and sometimes unpleasant, is one way to develop a closer relationship with the CaredFor. It moves the attention away from what is being done.

In the case of the P-Dance, it not only brought us closer together. It made my mother laugh. As a CareGiver, never pass up an opportunity for a good laugh.

Laughter reduces stress. Laughter improves the immune system's response. There are many other well-documented benefits to laughter. If you can find things to laugh about, it will make the first days of being together easier. It may not lead to Easy Street, but as the song says, "when life looks like Easy Street, there is danger at your door." What does that mean in the context of care giving?

Stay alert. Stay attuned to the present moment[1]. Conditions can change quickly in the life of the CaredFor.

If I wasn't paying attention, my mother could have lost her balance, fallen and hit her head on something. She may even have broken a bone in the fall.

This indeed happened the first time I had to leave my mother alone when I was out of town on a scheduled trip. I had arranged for a home care worker to spend nights with her while I was away. I had the home care worker come over the night before I left to see how my mother would react. My mother stayed awake for most of the night. She wasn't comfortable with a 'stranger' sleeping in the apartment with her.

I left the next day, despite my misgivings about her inability to sleep with the home care worker in the apartment.

The first morning I was away, I got a call from the home care worker telling me that she found my mother lying on the floor of her bedroom. My mother had reached up to get her robe off the hook on her closet door. She lost her balance and fell. She fractured her pelvis.

It doesn't take but a moment to convert a normal day into a chaotic one.

In the first days of care giving, look around to see what might be hazardous conditions. If you are introducing home care workers into the home environment, stay around until the CaredFor gets comfortable with the non-family member being around.

As you begin your role as a CareGiver, keep in mind the lessons from the opening lines of "Uncle John's Band."
1. "The first days are the hardest days" as you start a new relationship with the Cared For.
2. Stay alert, stay attuned to what is happening, because "when life looks like Easy Street, there is danger at your door."
3. And most importantly, "are you kind?"

Laying the foundation of a being compassionate presence at the start of your relationship with the CaredFor will go a long way to reducing the stress level in care giving and becoming a CareGiver. In the next chapter, we'll talk about how to become a compassionate presence.

Chapter 3 Becoming a Compassionate Presence

Presence is an experience, not just an idea in the mind. In fact, the mind of itself cannot be present (take my word for that!). The mind can only reprocess the past, judge the present, and worry about the future. Only some form of meditation will teach you how to move from an egocentric, fear-based life to a love-based life. Instead of splitting and dividing up Reality according to your preferences, you are able to see and enjoy everything that is—and as it is.

>Richard Rohr, O.F.M.
>Adapted from Contemplation and Non-Dual Consciousness
>(an unpublished talk given in Tucson, Arizona)

For CareGivers, there always seems to be something 'to do.' The realm of doing is what is familiar to CareGivers. The most important lesson I learned during the time I spent caring for my mother was a lesson she taught me.

It wasn't something she taught me explicitly. She wasn't even aware she was teaching me a lesson. I didn't recognize that she was teaching me a lesson. Not until I reflected on what she said did I realize how important were her words.

What she taught me is that the essence of care giving is being a compassionate presence in the life of another.

Let me tell you the story of how I learned this lesson.

One troubling symptom of mom's liver disease was that her body filled with fluids. The medical term for this symptom is ascites. Her legs would swell first. Then, fluids built up in her abdomen. It made her look like she was 6 months pregnant.

About every 3 weeks, I would have to take her to the emergency room to get the fluids drained. It wasn't an emergency when it was time to have the fluids drained. But it was easier to get her admitted to the hospital by taking her to the emergency room than it would have been if her doctor had to arrange for her admittance to the hospital.

It was one of the tricks you learned as you became an experienced CareGiver. I got to know well the triage process of hospital emergency rooms.

One evening, my mother was sitting quietly at the end of the long sofa in the living room. Fluids had been building up. It would soon be time to take her to the emergency room once again to have the fluids drained.

I came over and stretched out on the sofa and rested my head on her swollen abdomen. A minute or two passed. Then mom began to stroke the hair on my head as she did when I was a little one. But back then, there was more hair on my head. She began to speak as she continued to stroke my hair.

Her voice was soft. As she spoke, her voice began to waver. I could hear the tears in her voice as she said to me: "Richard, I don't know what I would have done if you weren't here."

I didn't say a word. I didn't even look back up at her. I continued to lay there. I let her regain her composure before I got up from the sofa.

Her words touched me deeply. If I had ever doubted my decision to quit my job to come back home to care for her, these words put any doubts to rest.

I noticed she didn't thank me for anything that I did. I knew she appreciated whatever I did for her, even when what I did may have caused her pain. For example, I insisted she take milk thistle, an herbal supplement that supports the health of the liver. The supplement came in a large capsule. She referred to it as a 'horse pill.' It was hard for her to swallow that capsule. She took it, nonetheless.

I noticed that what she did express appreciation for was my presence. It didn't occur to me how vulnerable she was. Knowing that there was someone there to look out for her was a real comfort.

It became clear to me that the essence of caregiving is being a compassionate presence. It is not about the doing. It is about how you are being. How you are being will inform your doing.

What do I mean by that? The attitude you have while doing the tasks of caregiving will affect the person you are caring for. If you feel obligated to be there, if you feel like you got stuck being the caregiver, the person you are caring for will feel it.

It is important to be present with the CaredFor, to be a compassionate presence as well as being a compassionate listener. I will address compassionate listening in the next chapter.

Learning to be a compassionate presence allows the CareGiver to be with the CaredFor in the present moment, without agendas, projections, or expectations. Becoming compassionate is a skill. Like any skill, the more often you practice it, the better you become at it.

Compassion is the attitude that enables you to be with a person. It is an attitude you can learn to cultivate. The dictionary defines compassion as sympathetic consciousness of others' distress together with a desire to alleviate it. http://www.merriam-webster.com/dictionary/compassion

Notice that both words, companion and compassionate begin with 'com,' the Latin preposition for 'with'. Every part of the CareGiver journey is about 'being with' – being with the person, the pain, the possibilities for a life interrupted by a dis-ease.

I write the word disease with a hyphen to emphasize that at the core of most illnesses there is a fundamental imbalance. The mind, body, and spirit are no longer at ease.

Compassion, according to the Buddhist tradition, begins with being kind to or friendly with one's self. As you develop this attitude of "friendliness toward oneself," you can extend this attitude to another and eventually to everyone, to everything and to every circumstance. In Sanskrit, the term for "friendliness toward oneself" is *maitri*.

A constant on the journey of care giving is pain. One way we can learn compassion is by examining our relationship with pain. This examination can lead us to a deeper understanding of our attitude toward ourselves. It is part of adopting the attitude of *maitri*. As we develop that attitude, or see what prevents us from holding that attitude, we will have a greater capacity to be compassionate with another. (We'll talk more about pain and suffering in Chapter 8.)

Compassion is a selfish skill. As I put it "You can't care for another unless you care for yourself...first!" The more you come to grips with who you are, your strengths and weaknesses, what some call your 'shadow self', the easier it becomes to relate to another. In the context of care giving, the other is the CaredFor.

Pema Chödrön, a Tibetan Buddhist nun, teaches a meditation practice called *tonglen*. In the booklet that accompanies the CD set called **Good Medicine**, *How to Turn Pain into Compassion with Tonglen Meditation*[1], she explains the principles of *tonglen*.

As Chödrön explains, "*Tonglen* (taking and sending) meditation" is the most immediate and direct way to cultivate genuine compassion. This "good medicine" can only be made from the poisons of anger, grasping, and ignorance. The transformative practice of *tonglen* turns these roots of anguish into a potent remedy that can heal the suffering of all beings.[2]

In my time as a care giver for my mother, I experienced the 'three poisons.' I got angry with a medical system that wouldn't allow my mother to be placed on the liver transplant list. I grasped at bits of information which I hoped would help my mother deal better with her symptoms. I was ignorant of how to maintain an attitude of compassion. There were many days when compassion was not *my* way of being.

During my time as a CareGiver, I did have a regular meditation practice. It did provide solace and strength in ways I did not understand but which I felt. The mediation practice I followed is called Centering Prayer. (see Chapter 5). I had not yet learned about the *tonglen* meditation practice.

Whether you adopt the *tonglen* meditation practice or not is clearly up to you. However, I strongly recommend that every day that you are a CareGiver set aside periods of silence. Meditation is a good way to spend those periods of silence. A CareGiver needs times of silence to get away from the demands of care giving. That said, let us explore *tonglen* further.

How to Practice *Tonglen*

Silence and breathing are at the heart of any meditation practice including *tonglen*. Here are a few guidelines that are helpful when you meditate.

Find a silent place where you won't be disturbed for at least 20 minutes. Turn off the TV or radio. Turn off your computer or tablet. Silence your cell phone. You may use your cell phone as a timer so long as the alarm is a gentle sound. You don't want to end your meditation time with a jarring sound.

If you are in a room with a door, close the door. Some prefer a darkened room.

Find a comfortable position that will allow you to breathe easily. Sitting in a chair with your back erect and your hands on your lap or by your side is a good beginning posture.

You can lie down, but for most of us, that is a signal for the body to fall asleep. So, I would not recommend that position when you are starting to meditate.

To avoid distractions in the room, close your eyes. If this causes you to tend to fall asleep, then close your eyelids almost all the way so that all you see is an area right in front of your feet. Some find it helps to focus on a single object like a candle.

Set your timer for 20 minutes, the recommended length of a meditation session. When you are starting out, you may only be able to sit for 5 or 10 minutes. Build up to 20 minutes.

Here are specific guidelines for the *tonglen* practice. When you begin your *tonglen* session, your intention is to take on the suffering of a person you know who is suffering. It could be the person you are caring for or another. It can even be you.

As you begin, focus on your breathing. Breathe in slowly through the nose filling your diaphragm. Avoid the shallow breathing common to our daily lives when we only fill the top of our lungs.

If you notice your shoulders or chest rising and falling as you breathe, you are shallow breathing. When you are breathing properly, you'll notice that only your stomach is rising and falling, not your shoulders or chest.

Then slowly exhale through your mouth. Some mediators exhale through their noses. Choose what is more comfortable for you.

There are four stages to *tonglen*. In the first stage, begin to relax your mind by observing what you are thinking. Don't judge your thoughts, just notice you are having thoughts.

In the second stage, focus on your breathing. This is your intention as you breathe in and out: *"The suffering of self and others is taken in with the in-breath; relief is offered with the out-breath to whoever needs it."*[3] In most cases, this other person is the CaredFor. But it could be another person you know who is suffering.

"This is the core of the practice: breathing in others' pain so they can be well and have more space to relax and open; and breathing out, sending them relaxation or whatever you feel would bring them relief and happiness."[4]

In the third stage, you become aware of the person or situation you are holding in your intention as you began breathing in and out. If this seems overwhelming, simply notice that this is a situation you are going through and that there are others who are going through the same circumstances.

You are not trying to fix anything or come up with solutions to the situation. You are simply noticing that you are not alone in your suffering.

You continue with breathing in the 'suffering of self and others' and extending 'relief to whomever needs it' as you breathe out.

At some point, you move into the fourth stage. It may be 5 minutes or 10 minutes later; there is not a specific time to begin the fourth stage. In this stage, you extend your intention to everyone, anywhere in the world who is in the same situation. You continue until your timer goes off.

Then gently bring your awareness back into the room. That's it. It's a simple practice: sit and breathe. When you start your practice, you may find it hard to sit for 20 minutes. Commit to sitting for at least 5 minutes and build up to 20 minutes. If you continue each day, you will find that you are able to sit for 20 minutes or more.

While you are seated, focus on the breathing in and breathing out. Don't worry about doing it wrong. Sit. Breathe in and out with the intention of breathing in suffering and extending relief as you breathe out. That's it.

The only thing that you can do 'wrong' is to get up and leave. If you fall asleep, that's OK. You needed the rest.

This form of meditation helps you become more compassionate as you focus on the suffering of another and extending relief. Whether you are aware of it or not, as you consistently practice *tonglen*, it shifts your attitude outside of your meditation time. You'll develop a capacity to be more compassionate, more patient, and more loving with those around you, particularly the CaredFor.

If you already have developed a meditative practice, continue with it. You can incorporate the intentions of the *tonglen* practice into your practice.

Whatever you decide, do consider making meditation part of your care giving practice. You can learn more about the importance of integrating meditation into your daily schedule in the book, **When Things Fall Apart: Heart Advice for Difficult Times.**[5]

Developing the capacity of compassion is essential to reducing the stress level of being a CareGiver. As you develop the capacity to be more compassionate, the less the day-to-day challenges will disturb your inner peace.

The capacity for being a compassionate presence is like a well. Dealing with the events of the day will draw down the level of the well. It needs to be refilled. The practice of daily meditation refills the well.

Schedule your periods of meditation as you would schedule any other important activity of CareGiving. If it's not on your schedule, likely you won't remember to do it. The recommendation is once in the morning and once in the evening.

Don't let your well run dry!

Chapter 4 "But I Gotta Do Something" …Yes, Listen

In the previous chapter, we looked at why being a compassionate presence is an essential skill for a CareGiver to develop. Compassionate listening is another essential care giving skill.

Compassionate listening is listening in a way which allows the CaredFor to have the experience of being heard. It is one of the greatest gifts a CareGiver can give. The CaredFor wants not only to know, but to feel there is someone there who cares, no matter what. The CaredFor is in a vulnerable position because his care depends on another. Knowing that the CareGiver is listening to his concerns is of great comfort to the CaredFor.

As the treatment for the disease progresses, the CaredFor begins to feel that everyone is trying to 'fix' him. The CaredFor loses his identity as a person. Instead, he becomes 'the one with a disease.' People begin to relate to the CaredFor as 'the problem to fix.' Some people may avoid the CaredFor even if the disease is not contagious.

The disease begins to define the identity of the CaredFor. The CaredFor starts to feel as though his interactions with others only occurs if it has something to do with managing his disease.

Compassionate listening is a way to give the CaredFor the sense that she is still a person with needs, wants, and desires like anyone else. The CaredFor is not the disease. The CaredFor is not diseased.

Developing compassionate listening

Compassionate listening is listening to understand the other rather than listening to respond to the other. Most of the time when we are in a conversation, as we hear what the other person is saying, we are preparing how we are going to respond. We are hearing, but we are not listening.

Throughout my life, friends would remind me that I have two ears and one mouth for a reason: to remind me to listen twice as much as I speak. If I am doing most of the talking, what can I possibly learn from and about the other person? Nothing. This is particularly good advice when you are beginning to practice the discipline of compassionate listening.

Compassionate listening is a discipline. It requires that you practice it regularly.

As a compassionate listener, the CareGiver learns to be aware of any expectations the CareGiver may have about care giving and the CaredFor. The CareGiver might be hoping for a cure. The CareGiver might be expecting the CaredFor to eat healthfully, to stop smoking, or to lose weight. The CareGiver might be expecting a specific response from the CaredFor, such as appreciation, gratitude, or compliance.

In becoming a compassionate listener, the CareGiver learns to let go of expectations before beginning a conversation with the CaredFor. Otherwise, these expectations will shape the conversation and become a filter through which the Care Giver listens to anything the CaredFor says.

Compassionate listening demands that the CareGiver be aware of any agendas the CareGiver has before having a conversation with the CaredFor. Is the CareGiver attempting to convince the CaredFor to do something or to change a behavior? Does the CareGiver want to change the care giving process? Is the CareGiver working to achieve a specific outcome? As with expectations, having an agenda in mind will shape and filter the conversation with the CaredFor.

For example, the CareGiver might begin a conversation about moving into an assisted living facility with the hope that this time the CaredFor would agree to move. If there isn't openness to listening to what the CaredFor is saying, there is no room for the CareGiver to consider other possibilities the CaredFor might suggest. In this conversation, all the CareGiver is open to hearing is that the CaredFor is finally ready to move into an assisted living facility. The expected outcome of the conversation already exists in the mind of the CareGiver. The CareGiver really can't hear anything else the CaredFor might say.

Even if the CareGiver does not mention a specific agenda item in a conversation, having it in mind does indeed shape the conversation. Intuitively, the CaredFor senses something else is going on in the conversation beyond the words being spoken.

The essence of compassionate listening is to be present to what the CaredFor is saying with nothing added or taken away. In other words, the CareGiver becomes aware of selective hearing – filtering out whatever the CareGiver really doesn't want to have to deal with.

This is a tall order. Just as it takes practice and training to become compassionate, as we saw in the previous chapter, it takes practice and training[1] to listen compassionately.

Here are a few tips to develop compassionate listening.

Compassionate listening is a listening without judging what the CaredFor is saying. The CareGiver stays connected to the present moment, not projecting into the future nor looking back at what has already happened. Otherwise, the CareGiver is hearing how **he** is being rather than being present to the way the CaredFor is showing up.

The compassionate listener learns to let go of judging as well as feeling being judged. As one friend quipped, "If you stop judging, you'll have a lot more time to do other things."

When we come to a conversation with an attitude of trying 'to fix' a situation, we really have no room to listen to the CaredFor. With this attitude, we are listening for an opportunity to propose our solution, rather than being open to discovering a solution that may already be present and within the CaredFor.

This is how a hospital chaplain, Rev. Lucy Sanders, describes the way she listens to her patients: *"As chaplains we get a chance to listen to a person for a long period of time, so that we can understand what they're looking for, and try to help them to tap into what's inside of them that is strong, that is calm, that is pretty stable, in a very chaotic environment. To help them think about what their resources are, what really matters to them, what's going to help them right now. I think that we are able to help a lot of people to find their own answers. We don't generally have answers. We ask questions, trying to keep people talking, and finding their own way."*[2]

Whether the CaredFor is at home, in a facility or in a hospital, the CaredFor has a need to be in control. When under care, someone is always telling them what to do. Someone tells the CaredFor when to wake up, when to eat, when to sleep, and what activities are on the schedule for the day. The CaredFor feels like she is no longer in control of her life.

As a CareGiver, if you come to a conversation with an intended outcome, you are intending to control the conversation with the CaredFor. The conversation then becomes one more area in which the CaredFor feels a loss of control.

In this context, you will feel the resistance from the CaredFor to anything you say. The resistance is not necessarily to the specifics of what you are saying, though that could be the case. The resistance by the CaredFor is to the feeling of being controlled.

How do you overcome this resistance? First, don't attempt to overcome the resistance. Your conversation with the CaredFor is not a battle. It is not your will versus his will. It is not about overcoming anything. It is about letting go of your desire to be in control so that you can be fully present to the CaredFor. It is a letting go of your agenda and your expectations of what should or shouldn't occur. Become open to what is.

Why all this concern with what the CareGiver is thinking about while listening to the CaredFor? Thoughts are not passive. Thoughts carry an energy that moves out into the world. The CaredFor, consciously or unconsciously, receives the energy of the thoughts of the CareGiver. Thus, it is important for the CareGiver to manage his thoughts before and during a conversation with the CaredFor.

When you aren't the right person for the conversation.

A challenging component of compassionate listening is to recognize when you may not be the best person to be having the conversation about a certain topic with the CaredFor.

The value of having a resource like a chaplain as part of your care giving team is that you can use the chaplain when, you the CareGiver, may not be the best person to discuss an issue with the CaredFor.

Consider this situation involving a woman who was the CareGiver for her mother. Her mother had been in hospice for several months. One day the mother calls the daughter and tells her, "I failed hospice." By this she meant that she had lived longer than the six-month period of her hospice care. Every six months, the hospice group must reevaluate the patient.

The mother left hospice care and returned home. Sometime thereafter, the mother went back to the hospital under hospice care. Based on her physical condition, the mother should have died by this point. Someone suggested that the mother talk with the hospice chaplain.

In the conversation with the chaplain, it came out that the mother was afraid that her daughter would not do well without her. She was staying alive for the sake of her daughter. The chaplain helped her understand that her daughter would be fine without her. Though the daughter had tried to reassure her mother that she would be fine after she died, her mother was not convinced. Hearing it from the chaplain made all the difference.

Before the chaplain reached his car on his way out of the hospital, the woman died. No matter how much the daughter had tried to tell her mother she would be fine after she died, the mother couldn't get that in her conversations with her daughter. So, despite her condition, she did whatever she could to stay alive for the sake of her daughter.

Becoming aware that you are not the best one to talk about a subject with the CaredFor is part of what it takes to become a compassionate listener.

Now that we have covered the two fundamental skills of becoming a compassionate CareGiver, compassionate presence and compassionate listening, we'll examine other skills 'to reduce stress and avoid burnout.'

I offer this poem as a reminder not to fall quickly into the "temptation of doing."

Intentionally Doing Nothing

Intentionally doing nothing is:
Noticing a long-tailed bird
       land on a branch,
Watching a dragonfly flutter –
       dare I call it a dance?
Observing the bend in a river
       through a wrought-iron fence,
Listening to a bird
       whose chirpings are intense.

Intentionally doing nothing is:
To see
       without looking,
To listen
       without hearing,
To speak
       without talking,
To run
       without racing,
To do
       without acting,
To surrender
       without giving up.

Intentionally doing nothing
is learning to just be.

Richard Anastasi
October 3, 2011
Irving, TX

Chapter 5 Starting With the End in Mind

We fear nothingness. That's why we fear death, of course, which feels like nothingness. Death is the shocking realization that everything I thought was me, everything I held onto so desperately, was finally nothing (read Kathleen Dowling Singh's **The Grace in Dying**).

Richard Rohr, O.F.M.
Adapted from **Radical Grace: Daily Meditations**,
p. 333, day 344

Asking the Questions about Dying and Death.

Part of the current paradigm of care giving is that death is a problem. It is something to prevent. It is something to fix.

Death is something that we fear mostly because we don't know what's on the other side of death. Nothingness? Eternal punishment? Eternal bliss? A return to take another chance to get it right?

Regardless of what you believe about what happens after death, there is a cultural uneasiness with dying and death. Existential philosophers and writers call this uneasiness 'angst. '

I say that until you can look death in the face and laugh, it will be your silent partner in your business of living life. Culturally, we have so much heavy baggage associated with death. It is no wonder that we want to avoid the subject. The next time you are at a social gathering, see how quickly people move away from you if you bring up the subject of death.

Have you ever tried to engage family members in a serious conversation about death? Was it easy to start the conversation? Were you able to start the conversation at all? Is so, how long did it last? Did you learn what their last wishes were?

If your family is like most families, this is not an easy conversation to have. Yet, it is a necessary conversation to have if you want to have any hope of being an effective CareGiver. How can you care for someone whose death is imminent if you have no understanding of how they feel about dying and death? Do they want to be kept alive at all costs? Do they value quality of life over quantity of life? Do they want to be buried or cremated?

These are just a few of the questions you need to ask and have answered if you are a CareGiver. By the way, you should have answered these questions for yourself, first. Make sure you have shared the answers with those you love. They might become your CareGivers at some point.

There is a wonderful booklet that can help you start this conversation about death with a loved one. It is called "The African-American Spiritual and Ethical Guide to End-of-Life Care" by Gloria T. Anderson[1]. In the Resources section at the end of this book, I have shared a link to a website where you can order it. Though it was written to address an African-American audience, its message is universal.

Another tool to use to help you start talking about end-of-life issues is "The Conversation Project"[2]. While well-known author, Ellen Goodman, was the CareGiver for her mother, she never had 'the conversation' about end-of-life issues with her. When her mother died, Goodman had to guess what her mother would have wanted. To make sure this didn't happen to other CareGivers, Goodman started The Conversation Project.

You can download a kit from The Conversation Project website to document your own end-of-life desires. (See the **Resources** section for details.)

As a CareGiver, you don't want to be in the position of having to guess about the desires of the CaredFor. Having to guess increases the stress of being a CareGiver.

Attitudes about Dying and Death

We don't think ourselves into a new way of living; we live ourselves into a new way of thinking.

The Eighth Core Principle:
The Center For Action And Contemplation

Asking and then developing answers to questions about dying and death is the first step toward developing a healthy attitude toward death. The next step is to reexamine your attitudes about dying and death. Move away from thinking about dying and death as you would think about learning to drive. When you learn a skill like driving, you learn to do it one step at a time. Do this first, then, do that, and then the next step. It is a logical and linear progression from one step to another. This is not the way to go about thinking about dying and death.

Thinking about dying and death requires an opening of the mind and heart to consider what already is: dying and death are going on within you and all around you all the time.

There are cells in our bodies dying every second of the day. It's in our DNA. Cells divide, creating new cells, which grow, decay, and then die. Our blood supply renews every seven years. There are multiple 7-year cycles going on within us.[3]

If we look at what happens as the seasons change, we see other cycles of birth, growth, decay and death repeating in nature. Consider the change in the color of the leaves on the trees each autumn. The leaves go from the color of birth and growth, green, through a range of yellows, oranges, and reds as the leaves decay, die, and then fall off their branches. Astronomers report the births and deaths of stars and galaxies. Even our own Sun is undergoing this cycle. At some point, it too, will run down and die out.

So why do we get upset or seem surprised when we encounter the cycle of birth, growth, decay, and death in ourselves or in loved ones?

As you observe the cycles of growth and dying that are going on within you and outside of you, take notice of what you believe, think, and feel about these cycles. Where did these beliefs, thoughts, and feelings come from? What are the habits and practices that accompany these beliefs, thoughts, and feelings? Have you consciously chosen them, or have you adopted and absorbed them from your parents, your teachers, and your culture?

Have you ever stopped to examine them? Do these attitudes toward dying and death still serve you or is it time to let go of them?

It is awkward to even begin a conversation about the end-of-life wishes of a parent or a spouse. Yet this is a necessary conversation to have despite the awkward feelings.

The attitude of 'letting go.'

It helps if you can let go of the attitude that death is a problem to fix. Rather, see it as part of the cycle of life. Are you open to the possibility that you can die right now rather than pretending death is out there in some vague time in the future?

The attitude of 'letting go' is a good one to adopt. Letting go is, in a sense, a form of dying. Letting go prepares us for the ultimate process of dying we call death. Katherine Dowling Singh describes well this attitude of letting go in her in her book **The Grace in Aging**[4]. When we can place our dying and death in the context of the larger cycles of our universe, it is easier to accept the reality of death. Death isn't something to postpone, ignore, or fight against.

Thich Nhat Hanh, a Vietnamese Buddhist monk, teacher, author, poet, and peace activist puts it this way in his book, **No Death, No Fear**: "when the conditions are right, spirit enters into the body. When those conditions no longer exist, spirit leaves the body."[5]

There is a transition of the spirit entering the body. We label that 'birth.' There is a transition of the spirit leaving the body. We label that 'death.

Our culture treats the transitions differently. From a spiritual point of view, you can label both transitions as births. From this point of view, there is no death. There is no final ending. This is what we fear about death, that it is the end. Thich Nhat Hanh is telling us we are holding onto a limited view of what death is. From his point of view, there is no death, just a transition to another form of life. Thus, as he writes, "no death, no fear."

Having a fear-less attitude toward death is a necessary attitude to reduce the level of stress in the life of a CareGiver. Once we put aside the attitude that 'death is a problem to fix', we are freed to explore the possibilities of life. As CareGivers, we can focus on developing a relationship with the CaredFor that aims at *the quality* of life, not the quantity of life.

There is another way in which we can learn to die. We die when we let go of what we think life is all about. We die when we let go of our idea of self (self with a small 's'). All our life we have lived as if the purpose of life is about acquiring things to make us feel happy, secure, or powerful.

Our life has a larger purpose. On the journey of CareGiving we will encounter situations where we come face to face with the bigger questions of life: Who am I? Where am I going? Why am I here?

When we have a job, or are building a career, we identify who we are by what we do. We associate where we are going relative to building the vision of our company. Usually we don't ask why. When asked, we might say: "to earn a living."

If you have not already confronted these questions, at some point in your role as a CareGiver, these questions will surface. If this doesn't happen while you are a CareGiver, watch for these questions to come up when your role as a CareGiver ends.

My purpose here is to shift your attitude towards the journey you are taking with the CaredFor. I want you to shift the primary focus away from considering only what there is to be done. I want to open your mind and heart to consider the fullness of life, for you and the CaredFor, even when there is suffering and hardship all around you.

Meditation: An essential tool for CareGivers.

An essential tool to developing an open mind and heart is the daily practice of meditation. Meditation will assist you in opening your mind and heart. We covered one form of meditation, *tonglen*, in Chapter 3. It comes from the world of Buddhism. There is another form of meditation from the Christian context called Centering Prayer. It was that meditation practice I was using during the time I was caring for my mother and still use today.

Father Thomas Keating, founder of Contemplative Outreach, introduces the practice in his book **Open Mind, Open Heart.**[6]

Tonglen helps you develop an attitude of compassion. Centering Prayer has a broader context. It opens you to the action and presence of God within you. Over time, it can help you let go of what Keating calls the "emotional programs for happiness."[7] These emotional programs for happiness keep us rooted in an attitude that we must do something to find happiness; that we must do something to be secure; that we must be in control of our lives; and that we need to have things to be happy. These attitudes make it difficult for us to see the fullness of life in just being alive.

When we are close to death, we can put into perspective the value of having things and the striving to acquire and protect them. We can let go of our attachments to possessions. We can even let go of attachment to our relationships. Detachment frees us from the fear of losing what we possess. In this way, we can face death free of attachment to this world.

The less attached we are to the things of this world, the easier is it will be to make the transition to whatever is next.

Adopting this attitude, we'll make the journey of care giving less stressful for both the CareGiver and the CaredFor.

Chapter 6 The Healing Power of Place

In this chapter, I will discuss a factor that is not usually discussed when considering where the CaredFor lives. It can have significant impact on the well-being of the Cared For. This factor is the 'power of place.'

Esther Sternberg, a neuro-immunologist, in her book **Healing Spaces: The Science of Place and Well Being,** documents the role 'place'[1] plays in creating stress or fostering healing. She is research director at the Arizona Center for Integrative Medicine at the University of Arizona. She was formerly at the National Institutes of Health where she did ground breaking research showing the link between the brain and rheumatoid arthritis.

In her book, Sternberg shares her own story of how a healing place helped her overcome the onset of disease. Ironically the disease was rheumatoid arthritis.

The role of place is important in care giving. Sternberg notes that a patient's interest in outside surroundings is the first indicator that healing is beginning. Sternberg's connection to place began early in her life. Her parents explicitly instilled in her at an early age that she should look, hear, smell, touch everything in her surrounding environment and savor it because this could be her last day. "Look at the sunset as if it's your last."

I had the privilege of meeting Dr. Sternberg at a conference in 2010 in Procida, Italy. She told us about a 1984 study by Roger Ulrich called "View from the Window." (See Chapter 1 of her book **Healing Spaces, The Science of Place and Well Being**.[2])

The study charts the progress of patients who underwent surgery at a facility that specialized in gall bladder surgery. Typically, it took several days for the patients to recover after the surgery.

The study examined data about the patients during recovery, such as how much pain medication the patients needed during recovery, how long they had to stay in the hospital, i.e. how quickly they healed, and the number of negative nurses' notes which documented that the patient was complaining about pain.

There were controls for factors such as age, sex, other medications, other diseases the patients had. All the patients had the same doctors and nurses, so the care was consistent. It was a well-controlled study.

What Ulrich's study found was that the significant variable in the patients' recovery was the view outside their windows. The study found that the patients who had a view of the grove of trees, on average, left the hospital a day sooner, needed less pain medication, and had fewer negative nurses' notes than those patients with a view of a brick wall.

The theory is that the part of the brain that recognizes beauty is also the part of the brain that releases endorphins. The release of endorphins promotes healing.

Whether circumstances dictate where the CaredFor lives or whether you have been able to plan for it, consider the role that healing spaces will have on the quality of life of the CaredFor.

[Some of the material in this chapter is based on an interview by Krista Tippett with Esther Sternberg on her radio show "On Being." [3]]

One of the biggest stressors for a CareGiver is finding the appropriate place for the CaredFor. The sooner the CareGiver discusses with the CaredFor where the CaredFor would like to live considering their medical conditions, the better. The goal of the discussion is to uncover not only what the CaredFor would like but also what the CaredFor would be willing to accept. While the CaredFor may want to continue living at home, the CaredFor might accept living in an apartment or at an assisted living facility.

A trend in elder care is 'aging in place.' Rather than moving the CaredFor to a facility to receive care, bring the care into the home of the CaredFor.

Before 'aging in place' became an accepted option, the typical progression of care began in the home. As the activities of daily living became more challenging, the CaredFor progressed through a series of facilities that offered more support and medical care. The progression usually ended with the CaredFor dying in a hospital bed. At each stage, the CaredFor was in less familiar surroundings reaching the point where they no longer felt 'at home.'

Keeping the CaredFor at home is a good place to begin care giving. It saves the CaredFor from the stress of moving and leaving a familiar environment. Unfortunately, it may not be possible or practical in all situations.

The CareGiver should work with the CaredFor to see whether the home is suitable for home care. Here are some questions to consider: Are doorways and hallways at least 36 inches wide? That is the minimum width needed to accommodate a wheel chair. Medicare won't pay for the cost of a wheel chair if the living area does not meet the 36-inch minimum requirement for halls and doorways.

If the bedrooms are on an upper floor, is there an elevator or stair lift to transport the CaredFor?

Is the entrance to the home easily accessible? Would the CaredFor need to climb up stairs to get to the entrance? Are there other obstructions that would inhibit the CaredFor's access to the home?

Are there support-bars in the bathtub or shower?

These are just a few of the items to address to make it practical for the CaredFor to remain in the home. There may be solutions to these issues like adding a stair lift or a ramp to remove stairs as an impediment. But there may not be money available to make the modifications to the home.

When money is a consideration, consider reaching out to charitable organizations. There may be an organization organized specifically to address the disease afflicting the CaredFor which may offer support.

Even if the home meets the accessibility criteria to allow the CaredFor to remain at home, the CaredFor's home may be too far away from the family members who would be available to provide care.

Making the decision of 'where to live while under care' is stressful because of the number of factors to consider: the desires and comfort of the CaredFor; the dictates of the disease; the involvement of the CareGiver; what living places are available; and of course, the costs involved.

Don't let finances enter the initial conversation. If you do, you might unnecessarily limit choices because you think you can't afford it. First, find out what the CaredFor wants. Then figure out whether it is affordable. There may be resources available that you were not aware of at the time you are having this discussion

If it turns out that it is not practical or possible to keep the CaredFor at home, then begin to investigate alternatives:

>moving in to the home of a family member.
>senior care communities.
>assisted living facilities.
>nursing homes.
>memory care facilities.

The list grows as providers come up with different solutions. Dr. Atul Gawande discusses a few of these solutions in his book **Being Mortal**.[4]

Handling the issue of what's the best place for the CaredFor is a stressful issue for both the CareGiver and the CaredFor. How do you maintain the balance between what the CaredFor needs and wants and what is affordable? That's the challenge. Facing this challenge is an underlying cause of stress.

What the CaredFor wants may not always be what is possible to deliver, or it may not be in the CaredFor's best interest. Remember, by definition, what's in the best interest of the CaredFor is what the CaredFor says he desires and wants. Because the CaredFor wants it can be reason enough.

Who decides what's in the CaredFor's best interest? The CaredFor? The doctor? The CareGiver? Does it come down to what does health insurance, Medicare or private funds cover?

When does the decision get made? Ideally, the CareGiver and CaredFor have discussed this issue in the context of a care plan. A care plan is a set of guidelines and action steps the CaredFor has developed with the CareGiver to direct how the CaredFor wants to be cared for.

It is important to note that it is 'a' decision. It is not 'the' decision made once and for all. The best place for the CaredFor is something that requires reevaluation as circumstances change.

Some of the factors to evaluate in deciding the best place for the CaredFor include funds available to pay for care, the level of care required, the rate of progression of the medical condition, and the environment for daily living.

The CareGiver's role is to protect the rights of the CaredFor, not to do what is easy for the CareGiver or what is 'expected.' The CareGiver makes sure that the wishes of the CaredFor are respected and not to give into "what *they* say is the right thing to do."

There are service providers who are available to assist with the decision "Which is the best place for the Cared For?" (See the **Resources** section for details.)

One provider in Dallas with whom I'm familiar is Senior Living Specialists. Paul Markowitz founded this service after struggling to find where to place his mother when she was ill. Paul and his brother had such a hard time doing this, they decided there had to be a better way.

Paul's standard for identifying placement opportunities is whether he would be happy to have placed his own mother there.

Paul meets with CareGivers to learn their needs of his. Then he makes several scheduled and unscheduled visits to the prospective facility with the CareGivers to assist them in finding a suitable place for the CaredFor. As it says on the Senior Living Specialists website[5], Paul offers "FREE assistance in your Senior Living search."

Using an experienced service provider will help you to come to a better understanding of the factors that lead to a good choice.

Become a Compassionate CareGiver - Reduce Stress. Avoid Burnout.

Chapter 7 Stop Fixin' the Disease – Heal the Person

After a friend of mine got over the shock of learning that his mother had stage four pancreatic cancer, one of the first things he did was to learn as much as he could about the disease. He had heard that pancreatic cancer progresses aggressively. He felt as if he didn't have a moment to lose.

This is a typical reaction of a CareGiver: learn as much as you can about the disease and how to treat it. When my mother started showing symptoms of primary biliary cirrhosis, I began learning about the disease from her doctors. As the disease progressed, I read about the disease and the organ it affected – the liver.

Why do CareGivers want to learn about the disease? They hope against hope that they'll discover something that will 'fix the problem.' As CareGivers, we see a disease as a problem to fix.

This is the predominant attitude of our health care system. There's a disease. It is killing people. That's a problem. Let's fix it.

In 1971, President Nixon tried to fix cancer. He announced it was time to wage war against the disease. America had been good at winning wars like World War I and World War II. By this time, we had already split the atom and put a man on the moon. Surely, America could successfully wage a war against a single disease and defeat it, couldn't we?

We have seen how well this approach has worked in defeating cancer. It is time to change our approach to disease as a problem to fix.

Unfortunately for me, I persisted in 'the disease as a problem to fix' mode throughout the time I was caring for my mother. I pursued the path of learning about the disease and how to treat it. As I said, I learned about her disease, primary biliary cirrhosis, by discussing it with the doctors who were treating her and by reading about it in articles I found using the Internet. But I also learned about the disease in an unexpected way.

About two months before I took on the role of CareGiver full time, I was on a flight from Albany, NY to New York City. I was flying on a regional jet (translation – a small airplane). I had boarded early and had a window seat. This was unusual for me since I typically reserved an aisle seat when I traveled. A middle-aged man sat down next to me in the aisle seat.

After the plane took off, we started up a conversation. My seat mate was a doctor who only treated women with primary biliary cirrhosis. What were the odds of that happening, sitting next to an expert on the disease my mother had?

He described the usual progression of the disease. He told me he first detects primary biliary cirrhosis in women in their forties and fifties. Symptoms don't appear until 15 or 20 years later. Symptoms can be managed, but there is no cure for the disease other than a liver transplant.

This doctor completed the picture of primary biliary cirrhosis for me. He confirmed what my mother's doctor and specialists had told us.

With no cure available, the strategy was to focus on the symptoms which caused the most difficulty for my mother: ascites (fluids accumulating in the legs and the area around the abdomen), confusion (caused by a build-up of ammonia which the liver can no longer remove from the blood), and acid reflux. My job was to monitor the reoccurrence of these symptoms and report it to her doctor.

I got good at symptom management. By the time my mother died, I felt I knew as much about the disease as many health care professionals. Yet, I felt like something was missing. There must be something else I can do!

A context for healing.

What I was missing was a context of healing. I was brought up with the idea that if you looked good and felt good, you were probably in good health. Yes, I went for my annual check-ups to make sure everything was fine. Unless I felt pain somewhere, I assumed everything was OK.

I have since learned that by the time you feel pain, you may have already lost as much as 40% of the functionality of an organ. That was the way it was for my mother. By the time the symptoms of her liver disease manifested, the liver was too far gone to heal.

The World Health Organization defines health as: "Health is a state of complete physical, mental and social well-being and not merely the absence of disease or infirmity."[1] Health is about the ability of the body to heal. If we are healthy, we will be able to maintain our well-being.

Until I encountered Maximized Living™ Doctors, my approach to health care was to do what it takes to avoid disease. What Maximized Living™ Doctors taught me is to work on maintaining the body's ability to heal rather than trying to figure out how to avoid a disease.

I started seeing a Maximized Living™ Doctor at the end of 2009. Since then, I have learned to optimize my health by paying attention to what they call the "Five Essentials."[2]

The Five Essentials are Maximized Mind™, Maximized Nerve Supply™, Maximized Quality Nutrition™, Maximized Oxygen™, and Minimized Toxins™. Following this model of health, you work on maintaining health rather than fighting disease.

When you get sick, focus on what has compromised or blocked the healing power of the body. Work to eliminate that. Then, allow the healing power of the body to handle the disease and its symptoms.

This model produces results. It is not a hypothetical model or the latest fade in health care.

Had I known about Maximized Living™ Doctors would my mother not have succumbed to the progress of primary biliary cirrhosis? No one can say for sure. But what I do know is that Maximized Living™ would have given me a context for evaluating all the information I had gathered about the disease, and equally as important, a different context to deal with the symptoms of her illness.

Become a Compassionate CareGiver - Reduce Stress. Avoid Burnout.

Instead of focusing on symptom management, I would have worked to figure out what was blocking the ability of my mother's body to heal? Why was the liver no longer functioning? What was getting in the way of the liver's ability to heal?

What we had not considered was what Maximized Living™ Doctors calls Essential #5[3], Minimized Toxins™. Maybe the problem wasn't the liver. Maybe the problem was that my mother had accumulated so many toxins that there was no way for the liver to keep up. What was causing the build-up of toxins in the first place?

The approach her doctors had been taking was to look at replacing the diseased liver. They weren't looking at what had overburdened the liver. The assumption was that the disease began in the liver. They never asked whether the accumulation of toxins in the body over time had caused the liver to become diseased.

Maybe there were other detoxification organs in the body that weren't working. What about the kidneys, the lungs, the digestive system, or the skin? Along with the liver, these organs are the body's detoxification system. Was she sweating? Sweating is a type of detoxification. Research shows that cancer patients have difficulty sweating. No doctor told me to monitor her ability to sweat.

Looking back over her life, I remember my mother had problems with constipation. Her doctors treated the symptoms of constipation, but never really addressed why it was a chronic issue.

Figuring out what might have really been responsible for my mother's death is not why I am writing this chapter.

I am writing this chapter to shift the focus of the CareGiver and the CaredFor to consider a different health care model. With the health care model that Maximized Living™ Doctors teaches, the emphasis is on healing. Eliminate from the body what is getting in the way of the body's ability to heal.

Coming from a context of healing gives the CareGiver a way to assess how well the CaredFor is being treated. Are the doctors focused only on fighting the disease and its symptoms or are they also looking for what is missing in the body that has allowed the disease to manifest in the first place?

If you only treat the symptoms of a disease, but never get to the root cause, it's likely the disease will continue to plague the body. That's why after a surgery designed to eliminate a symptom of a disease, such as a tumor, the disease appears to come back. The tumor didn't cause the disease. Eliminating the tumor doesn't cure the disease. The removal of the tumor reduces the toxic load on the body. So, there is value to having the surgery. However, from my point of view, the surgery would have greater value if it was part of an overall strategy to improve the ability of the body to heal.

To see an example of the Maximized Living™ Doctors approach in action, read about how one of the Maximized Living™ Doctors, Dr. Charlie Majors, healed from stage four bone marrow cancer. Read the book Dr. Majors co-wrote, **The Cancer Killers.** (See the Bibliography.)

In it, he chronicles how he overcame his cancer without resorting to chemotherapy, radiation, or surgery. His treatment plan was an intensified form of following the Five Essentials.

I am an unabashed proponent of the Maximized Living™ Doctors model for health and healing. It's now the one that guides my health care decisions. It's a health care model that works. As a CareGiver, it is important to adopt a health care model that you believe in. As the adage goes, "If you don't stand for something, you'll fall for anything." As a CareGiver, it's important for you to adopt a health care model that works for you *and* the Cared For. It is the CaredFor whose life is at stake.

You cannot impose a solution on the CaredFor. Otherwise, the CaredFor will be fighting against the solution, reducing the chance of the solution succeeding.

Believing in a treatment method is important. As another adage goes, "Whatever one can conceive and believe, one can achieve."

Dealing with information overload.

Whichever model of health the CareGiver adopts, there is a continual challenge of keeping up with information about the disease. It is hard to know which information you can trust as you research the disease and the treatment of it. The best suggestion is to continue to track trusted sources, sources recommended by people you trust.

that provide research to support claims. The sources

Before proceeding, let's stop a moment to see where we are on the journey of care giving. In the Introduction, I told you I was writing this book from the perspective of being your CareGiver Guide, as one who has already made a care giving journey.

I promised to share insights with you that I believe would help a CareGiver to 'reduce stress and avoid burnout.' The Introduction, Chapters 1 and 2, set up the problem: the current paradigm of care giving is all about doing. Chapters 3 and 4 addressed how to shift the paradigm from doing to being by teaching you how to become a compassionate presence and a compassionate listener.

In Chapters 5 through 7, we examined specific strategies to reduce stress. Now we'll continue to explore strategies to reduce stress by showing the power of stories.

Chapter 8 Pain & Suffering

"Pain is the signal the body sends to our brain. **Suffering is the *story* we tell about our pain."**

Dealing with pain is an inevitable part of care giving. As human beings, we seek pleasure and avoid pain. The stress of dealing with pain comes from our desire to seek pleasure and avoid pain. Pain is part of the human condition. Attempts to resist pain do not lead to pleasure but to suffering.

A central tenet of Buddhism is that we suffer because we want the world to be the way it is not. If you are in pain, for you, that is the way the world is. Wishing it to be other than the way it is causes you to suffer.

Suffering is the story we tell about our pain. Pain is the body's way to inform us that something is not right. Pain signals us to move away from behaviors and conditions that are causing us pain. It signals a condition that the body, mind, or spirit is not at ease. In other words, we have a disease. ["Dis" is a prefix meaning 'not'].

The way to deal with pain is acceptance. Accept that we have pain. Don't try to mask over the pain, ignore the pain, or deny the pain. When we accept the pain, we are open to look for the causes of the pain, rather than merely to focus on the immediate symptoms of pain.

When I was 38, I developed a sharp pain in the area between my right hip and knee. I had just begun a physical fitness program. At first, I ignored the pain thinking it was part of the price of getting back into shape after years of not working out.

Finally, I went to see a doctor specializing in sports injuries. He suspected I had a 'bulging disc' which was putting pressure on the sciatic nerve. He sent me for a CAT scan. The neurosurgeon who reviewed my CAT scan told me that I would "be under the knife in about five years."

In the meantime, the suggestions to treat the symptom, the sciatic pain, were to rest, to ice the area after work outs, and to take Ibuprofen for the pain. I was told I had to deal with the pain until I had back surgery.

I chose instead to find out how to deal with the cause of the pain, the bulging disc putting pressure on the sciatic nerve. I went to see a chiropractor. After a few weeks of adjustments, the pain went away. I continued monthly maintenance treatments. It is over 25 years later. I don't have the sciatic pain and I never had to have back surgery as the neurosurgeon predicted.

The chiropractic adjustments were only part of the solution. I learned what was responsible for the bulging disc in the first place. It had to do with the sedentary nature of my job, sitting at desk in front of a computer terminal and on airplanes. My job required lots of travel. I didn't work out regularly, either.

The pain caused me not only to seek treatment but also to change my behavior. I began a regular practice of walking which helps with lower back issues. I learned about proper posture when sitting in front of a computer and on airplanes.

The pain was a signal to change my behavior and the conditions causing my pain. This was a straightforward case of pain management. Find the cause, treat the cause, and eliminate the symptom – the pain.

Not all cases of pain are this simple. With most diseases, the identification of the causes and the treatments are more complex. When pain is reoccurring, there is a psychological dimension of pain. Each time the stimulus for the pain occurs, we also recall what we experienced the last time we felt that stimulus. It becomes part of the story of that pain.

Think about your experience the next time you go for a blood test or donate blood. Don't you begin to tense up even before the nurse reaches for the needle? Why? Because you remember how it hurt the last time this happened and the time before that and the time before that.

I recall tensing up before an injection when I had to have blood drawn for a test. The nurse was so good at giving injections that I didn't even notice she had done it until after she pulled the needle out. I wasn't experiencing pain. I was suffering. I was suffering because of the story I was telling myself about what happens when you get an injection. I wasn't being present to what I was experiencing. I was stuck in the memories of what happened with previous injections.

Part of dealing with pain is being present to the pain you are experiencing now. Accept the pain the way it is now, not how it was the last time you experienced a similar pain, and certainly not how you might expect it to be. Does this make the pain any less painful? No. But it does reduce the suffering.

The suffering comes from what we add to the present experience of pain based on our memories. Suffering is the story which we tell about our pain. It is the story we tell ourselves which adds to our experience of the pain. No story, less suffering.

Pain management.

As a CareGiver, the problem of pain management is rife with suffering for the CareGiver. Why? The CareGiver gets to observe the pain the CaredFor is experiencing. The CareGiver is not experiencing the pain of the CaredFor. Yet the CareGiver suffers with the CaredFor. The CareGiver has 'a story' in mind about the pain the CaredFor is feeling.

All the CareGiver can know is what it *might* be like for the CaredFor based on the experiences of pain the CareGiver has known. What the CareGiver experiences is suffering, the stories or memories the CareGiver associates with pain. It could be based upon stories the CaredFor has been speaking about her pain. It could be based on the stories the CareGiver has read about the pain associated with a specific disease. Or it could be based on stories the CareGiver imagines about the pain.

What's a solution for the CareGiver? Don't get caught up in the drama of the situation and stick with the "facts." Recognize it is the CaredFor who is experiencing pain. Focus on that. As CareGivers, our job is to let go of our own experiences, memories, stories about pain and become present to the CaredFor.

My mother told me that morphine made her feel 'loopy.' That was her way of telling me and her doctor how morphine affected her awareness. Her doctor worked to find other pain killers which relieved the pain, but which wouldn't make her feel 'loopy.' I think she was willing to put up with a little more pain rather than to feel 'loopy.' That was my mother's choice. She wanted to maintain her awareness even if it came at the cost of more pain.

As her CareGiver, I could have insisted she take the morphine because it was more effective at relieving her pain. Why might I have done this? Because it might have made me uncomfortable to see her in pain. Fortunately, for my mother, at least in this case, I didn't impose what I wanted for her. I let her choose.

As CareGivers, it's best to put aside our stories about pain to stay open to discovering how the CaredFor is experiencing pain. Here are a few of the basic questions the CareGiver can ask the CaredFor about pain:

1. How intense is your pain? On a scale of 0 to 10 with 10 being excruciating pain and 0 being no pain at all, how do you feel? For those with limits on their verbal skills, you can show them a picture of a ruler with marks from 0 to 10 so they can point to the pain level. Some home care workers, whose responsibilities include pain management, carry with them a set of pictures depicting different levels of pain.

2. When have you taken your last pain medication? Have you been taking the medication at the prescribed times? Maintaining a specific level of pain medication in the system is essential for the pain medication to be effective.

3. Is your level of pain getting in the way of your ability to perform the tasks that are important to you? I believe this is one of the most important questions that the CareGiver can ask. The answer will help the CareGiver to understand how to support the CaredFor in achieving successful pain management. Hopefully there is a palliative care specialist available to assist with pain management.

Let's say the CaredFor says that it is important to be able to write to associates, family, and friends, and that a specific dosage of morphine makes him too drowsy to write. Yet, that dosage lowers his pain level. The CaredFor might agree to tolerate a higher level of pain (less pain medication) to maintain the ability to write.

Knowing the pain intensity and how much medication is needed to get to a tolerable level of pain is part of a pain management plan. The medical specialty dedicated to pain management is called palliative care.

Palliative Care

Palliative care specialists design treatment plans that seek to create a balance between alleviating pain and living consciously. The aim of palliative care is to make the CaredFor as comfortable as possible. It does not aim to cure a disease that is responsible for a pain. Yet, palliative care can be part of an overall treatment plan that does aim at curing the disease.

When curative treatment is no longer effective or if the CaredFor has decided to stop curative treatment, palliative care is still available to keep the CaredFor comfortable until the disease has run its course. The focus moves from curing the disease to maintaining quality of life.

This is an appropriate time to consider hospice care. Palliative care and hospice care are not interchangeable terms. Hospice care includes palliative care, but you don't have to be under hospice care to receive palliative care.

Palliative care is a way to enable the CaredFor to live life as fully and consciously as possible given the situation. An experienced palliative care team works with the CaredFor to find the amount of pain medicine which will relieve the pain yet have the least impact on the ability of the CaredFor do the things she enjoys.

What's the difference between palliative care and hospice care?

In the United States, to qualify for hospice care, two medical doctors must agree that there is a probability (not a certainty) that the CaredFor could die of a specific diagnosed disease within six months. If the patient is eligible for Medicare, Medicare will pay for most hospice care services. If not, private insurance or Medicaid may cover the cost of hospice care. Medicaid coverage varies by state. Eligibility will vary according to where you live.

Medicare and health insurance companies define which services they will cover as part of hospice care. Whatever is deemed to be curative treatment is not part of hospice care. Note that Medicare or your insurance policy won't cover everything just because you qualify for hospice care. However, the CaredFor can leave hospice care if he wants to resume curative care.

One of the goals of hospice care is pain management. Palliative care is the part of hospice care that addresses pain management. While as a medical specialty, palliative care is relatively new, the practice of palliative care goes back hundreds of years.

Thanatos Music

The Benedictine monks in Cluny, France practiced palliative care in the eleventh century. The Latin root of the word palliative is *'palliare'* which means 'to cloak.'

The monks used a combination of herbs and music to assist with a 'blessed death.' The scribes at the monastery recorded these practices which are referred to as the "Cluniac customaries."

Therese Schroeder-Sheker studied the Cluniac customaries and learned about the music the monks played. She is founder of the Chalice of Repose. From 1992 to 2002 she was the academic dean of the School of Music-Thanatology, which was housed at St. Patrick Hospital in Missoula, MT.[1]

In an interview[2], Therese Schroeder-Sheker tells how she uses Thanatos Music to ease the CaredFor through the process of dying. [Thanatos is the Greek word for death.] She makes it clear that she is not putting on a deathbed concert.

Thanatos Music[3] is different from music we usually listen to. It has no countable beat or meter. Much of the music we listen to has a 4/4 meter, 4 beats to the measure of music. A waltz has a 3/4 meter, three beats to the measure of music.

Thanatos Music has no meter. It is melodic but not metrical. There is something about non-metrical music that is soothing to the person in pain. Schroeder-Sheker describes Thanatos Music as prescriptive. That is, it is prescribed for an individual just as a medical doctor would prescribe pain medication for a patient. However, the Thanatos Music prescription is personalized for every individual. One size does not fit all.

For Schroeder-Sheker, Thanatos Music is both a medical and spiritual practice. While it eases pain, it also eases the suffering a patient may be undergoing as he or she faces death. As patients are letting go of their outer self - the way they look, who they were in life, their possessions, their relationships – they start to go inside and begin to work on issues of the inner-self such as forgiveness. Thanatos Music, according to Schroeder-Sheker eases the letting go associated with both the outer and inner self.

The application of music to relieving pain is not limited to the end-of-life period. Music therapy is one more tool a palliative care specialist can rely on in managing pain.

Music Therapy

Music therapy, like Thanatos Music, is another tool to use in managing pain and suffering. Music therapists are licensed professionals who apply music to treating pain.

There is a well-documented use of music therapy at the Cleveland Hospital as an alternative to morphine in treating burn wounds. Changing the bandages of patients with burn wounds is an extremely painful process. Typically, burn wound patients receive high dosages are narcotics to deal with the process of having their bandages changed. One burn wound patient reported that using music therapy while a nurse changed his bandages was the first time that was done without him feeling pain. According to him, music therapy provided better pain relief than morphine had.[4]

Palliative care is an essential part of managing those with chronic pain and particularly for those near death, who are dealing with pain and are no longer receiving curative treatment. A skilled palliative care practitioner is a great resource to have on the care giving team. Regardless how you treat the pain, remember the distinction between pain and suffering. Suffering is the story we tell about our pain.

Chapter 9 Grief & Loss

The grief process of a CareGiver is unique. When the person the CareGiver is caring for dies, the CareGiver has three losses to deal with. The first loss is the obvious loss, the loss of the person who has just died. The next two are not as obvious. One is the loss of the life the CareGiver might have had if he had not become a CareGiver. The other is the loss of the life of being a CareGiver.

Let's deal with the grief of the obvious loss.

Grieving for the loss of the CaredFor

When someone we care about dies, there is clearly a tangible loss of that person's presence in our life. When we come home at night, they are not there to welcome us. When we wake up in the morning, they are not there at breakfast. There are many ways in which the person we were caring for is no longer present in our life.

We mourn that loss. How we feel about this loss is what we call grief.

Grief is more than an emotion. Grief is a process. Unlike other processes that have a beginning, middle, and end, grief has a beginning, but it is hard to say when you are at the middle or at the end. For some, the pain of grieving may lessen, but the grieving never ends. Something that reminds the CareGiver of the CaredFor can rekindle the grief process. This is not necessarily a bad thing so long as the grieving isn't interfering with the CareGiver's ability to get on with life.

Elizabeth Kübler-Ross, in her book **On Death and Dying,** published in 1969, identified five stages of grief.[1] This is how David Kessler, who co-authored **On Grief and Grieving** with Kübler-Ross, describes the stages of grief on his website:

"The five stages, denial, anger, bargaining, depression, and acceptance are a part of the framework that makes up our learning to live with the one we lost. They are tools to help us frame and identify what we may be feeling. But they are not stops on some linear timeline in grief. Not

everyone goes through all of them or in a prescribed order. Our hope is that with these stages comes the knowledge of grief's terrain, making us better equipped to cope with life and loss. At times, people in grief will often report more stages. Just remember your grief is as unique as you are[2]*."*

As Kessler says, "the grief process is as unique as you are." Whether you go through all the stages of grief or just a few, what is most important is that you give yourself the time to grieve. The feelings associated with loss are real. You need time to process those feelings.

The process of grief gives you a way to deal with whatever feelings surface.

Some people deal with grief by talking to others about it. Others may write about it in a journal. Some seek the support of grief groups or grief counselors. Some do all three at once. For example, you might decide to first join a group. Then, within the context of the group, you might find a safe place to talk about your grief. The group counselor may encourage you also to write about it in a journal.

If you deny or hide your feelings, it is only a temporary solution. At some point, you will have to come terms with those feelings. The longer you wait, the harder it will become.

In early December of 1980, an oncologist at Mother Cabrini Hospital in New York City told me and my parents that my sister, Gloria, had adeno carcinoma. With treatment, she might live another six months. Hearing that death sentence, I cried.

Gloria died 8 months later. My father called me at work to tell me "our Pigeon is gone." He sometimes called her 'my little Pigeon.' I didn't shed a single tear. I didn't cry at the wake when friends and relatives came to pay her their respects. I didn't cry at the cemetery when they lowered her coffin into the ground.

It took six years before I finally mourned for Gloria. I was driving home after a business meeting in New York City. I cannot recall what triggered my tears, but from the time I got on exit 14C of the New Jersey Turnpike until I got off at exit 9, I cried without ceasing. It was after rush hour. As I recall, it takes about 30 minutes to drive from Exit 14C, Holland Tunnel/Jersey City to Exit 9, New Brunswick, NJ in non-rush hour traffic.

I had not taken the time to grieve right after Gloria died. I had stuffed down the feelings I was holding onto from the time I first heard she had only six months to live until that evening driving home. Those feelings eventually exploded in a flood of tears. I can't even begin to comprehend the toll this had taken on my life in the years in between.

As the spokesperson on an old commercial about car maintenance used to say, "You can pay me now, or, pay me later." It is the same with grieving.

When my mother died eighteen years later, I had learned my lesson. At the time of her death, she was under hospice care. A benefit of hospice care is that it includes grief counseling for the survivors. I took advantage of it.

I grieved differently for my mother than I did for my sister, Gloria. With the loss of my sister, I never made time to grieve. I quickly got back into the routine of work. I stuffed my feelings of grief.

With my mother, I immediately participated in the grief group that hospice directed me towards. Frankly, I found no immediate comfort in the sessions I attended. But I attended them religiously anyway. Why?

It gave me an opportunity to see how other people were handling the loss of their loved ones. It gave me an opportunity to be supportive to others in the group. I held out the hope that something would happen in the next session that would help me.

What I did find moving was a memorial service the hospice group at Beth Israel Hospital (where my mother died, now called Mt. Sinai-Beth Israel Hospital) held regularly in honor of those who had died at their hospice facility. It was a non-denominational 'religious' service open to the friends and family of the deceased. I found some comfort in this service which occurred several months after my mother died and after the grief group sessions had ended.

When I returned from New York City to my home in Texas, a friend in my Centering Prayer group told me about a grief group that was meeting at her church. I went to that as well. Again, I can't say that I felt comforted.

You might be wondering whether it is worthwhile to attend these groups. My instinct is to say 'yes.' Attend. You cannot judge ahead of time what will bring you comfort. Go with an open mind. If you go with the attitude 'this won't help,' guess what? It won't help. Yet, you never know.

Grieving is highly individual. What works for me may or may not work for you.

What I can say with confidence is that not making time to grieve is a source of stress for CareGivers. For a CareGiver, grieving does not start with the death of the CaredFor.

There is another type of grief the CareGiver experiences before the death of the CaredFor.

Grieving for the loss of a way life

As soon as person becomes a CareGiver, you consciously or unconsciously begin to grieve the loss of the way life used to be before CareGiving.

You may become resentful or even angry that life as a CareGiver required changes to your 'normal' way of living.

Pursuing a career while being a CareGiver will indeed impact your career trajectory. The demands of care giving make it difficult to devote the same number of hours to your career as you were used to devoting. If travel or working long hours are important to advancing your career, you may not advance as rapidly or at all. Or, as in my case, you might face the choice of whether to continue in your career or be a CareGiver.

Here are some questions you may be asking yourself as you process this type of grief.

"What would have happened if I did not have to choose between continuing in my job as before and becoming involved in care giving?"

"Where would I be in my career now and does that still matter?"

"Can I get back on the 'fast track'? Do I even care about being on the 'fast track' anymore?"

At first, you may not be asking yourself questions like these. At some point, you will. If you don't allow yourself time to process the emotions these questions evoke, it may prevent you from grieving the impact of your role as a CareGiver.

You may not like the answers you come up. Keep asking the questions. Why? To give yourself the chance to see the questions from different perspectives. Hopefully, you can shift your attention from what might have been to the opportunity you now have.

What opportunity? The opportunity to clearly look at your life to see if it is a life you have chosen or if it is a life you have settled for.

When you confront death daily as a CareGiver, it puts into perspective what really is important in life: learning to love yourself, your family of origin and family of choice, and the Source from which all love flows.

Grieving for the loss of being a CareGiver

Ironically, some CareGivers may experience grief over their loss of being a CareGiver. When you are a CareGiver, your life has intensity and a clear purpose. Care giving defines your daily routine. After the CaredFor dies or heals, as the CareGiver, you are no longer the essential person in the life of another. You no longer need to maintain the intense state of readiness as the CareGiver.

Some CareGivers experience this as a loss, a loss of an intensely personal relationship and a feeling of being wanted and needed.

As the CareGiver, you likely made life altering choices on behalf of the CaredFor. When you are no longer a CareGiver, it is unlikely that you will be expected to make life altering decisions for someone else. Your life won't be as intense. You may miss the intensity of life as a CareGiver and the intimate relationship with the CaredFor.

Regardless of which of these griefs you are mourning, you owe it to yourself to learn about the grief process, and to give yourself the gift of the time to grieve.

Let's review the three types of grief a CareGiver experiences: grieving the loss of the CaredFor, grieving the loss of the way life could have been had you not become a CareGiver, and grieving the loss of being a CareGiver.

As a CareGiver, you will go through cycles of grieving these three losses.

Grief is an emotion, but it is also a process. If you don't allow room for this process in your life, life at some point will make room for it in ways that are unexpected.

Do not allow anyone to tell you that there is a right way to grieve. Do give yourself the time to grieve. Do not push away, cover over, or stuff down your feelings of grief.

Though there is pain and suffering in grieving, I found grieving provided solace and a sense of unburdening a load which I wasn't aware I was carrying.

Embrace the process of grieving. It is worth the effort.

Chapter 10   Make Memories, Not Misery

It's late at night. All that could be done this day has been done or left undone. No cure is expected. No miracle hoped for. All is well at this moment. The CaredFor is not yet ready for bed, nor are you.

This is when I would ask my mother, "Do you want some tea or coffee?" I had already begun to boil water before I had asked. Either tea or coffee would be ready soon. I'd go to the big, round aluminum cake tin on the cabinet next to the kitchen stove and pull out a couple pieces of our favorite dessert, sfogliatella.

Even if she wasn't hungry, she'd have a piece. Sometimes, we'd talk. Mostly, we sat and ate with the late-night news droning on the television in the living room. Sometimes it was quiet...just the two of us munching on sfogliatella and sipping our coffee or tea.

Were caffeine and a sugary dessert the best thing for either of us to be consuming? Probably not. But at this point, did it really matter? The look of enjoyment on her face eating the sfogliatella made it a good idea from where I sat.

This is what I mean when I say, 'make memories, not misery.' I could have given her another pill for her health, but to what end? At this point she had difficulty swallowing the 'horse pills,' as she sometimes called her prescribed pills and supplements. Her liver wasn't going to heal, so why put her through further discomfort?

Do you do something like this every night? Do you totally give up on prescribed medicines or on a healthy diet?

No, to both questions, for both you and the CaredFor. As the CareGiver, you are responsible for maintaining your health. As the one responsible for the CaredFor, you don't want to do anything that will lead to increased pain or discomfort. Your intuition will let you know when a shared 'forbidden dessert' does more good than harm.

There's an ancient Greek adage, "All things in moderation – even virtue." Don't be afraid to indulge occasionally.

Sometimes, when my mother didn't want to share in the late-night snack, I think the smell of the coffee percolating on the stove was healing. Healing comes from within. The smell of coffee, I believe, evoked a pleasant sense memory. That pleasure supports healing.

That's not to say that if the CaredFor is diabetic that you would do something that intentionally would spike her sugar levels. Or, if the CaredFor enjoys drinking lots of coffee, be aware that the acid in the coffee might upset her stomach later. You should be prudent but not prudish.

I'm not saying throw caution to the wind and do whatever you want despite what your medical team has recommended. Ask them whether an occasional indulgence on the sweet side is tolerable or whether there's risk to indulge even a little. Ask. Weigh the risks and benefits. Just don't make it a research project that prevents you from deciding.

Time is precious, particularly when the end is near.

Looking back on the time I spent with my mother, I'm glad we had those late night 'coffee and dessert' breaks.

These 'coffee and dessert' experiences are part of what I call the participation aspect of care giving. As a CareGiver, it is important to engage in the life of the CaredFor.

It is one thing to buy the coffee and dessert and leave it for the CaredFor. It's quite another to buy the coffee and dessert and spend time sharing it together. The time spent sharing shows the CaredFor that you really are there for them. It demonstrates to the CaredFor that you are being a compassionate presence.

You can read about being compassionate. You can talk about being compassionate, but until you are *being* compassionate by sharing in the life of the CaredFor, you are missing the boat.

A football coach will tell you that a coach can't really begin to coach his players until they get out on the field and begin playing. Then the coach can see whether the player has just read the playbook or whether the player can execute what's in the playbook.

CareGivers, don't just read this book. Go out and play!

Never pass up the opportunity to share in the life of the CaredFor. You never get those moments back. Each opportunity is a chance to deepen your relationship, to express your love for the CaredFor.

Equally as important, it is a time for you to receive the love of the CaredFor. You may never hear the words "I love you." Actions speak louder than words. As one author has put it, "Love is a verb.[1]" Love is both a way of being and a way of doing.

Sharing quite time with the CaredFor gives you an opportunity to listen to what is on the mind of the CaredFor. It also gives you an opportunity to listen for what might be missing. Ask if there is something that the CaredFor would like or what might need adjusting. The room is too dark or too light, too hot, too cold, too noisy, too quiet. Maybe their pain medication needs adjusting.

When you are together, if you feel there is nothing to talk about, that's OK. Not every minute of your time together needs to be spent in conversation. If you want to spark a conversation, ask questions that require more than a 'yes' or 'no' reply.

Ask questions about the CaredFor's childhood. What was life like when the CaredFor went to school? Who was his best friend? Where is that friend now?

If the CaredFor is a parent, ask what were you like when you were little. Even if you have heard the stories before, listen to them as if you have never heard them. Indeed, you really have not. Each time you hear the story, you are a different person and so is the one telling the story.

Each time the CaredFor tells her story, there is the possibility that some new detail might come out that has been withheld up until now. The CaredFor might even change some of the details. As one hospice chaplain told me when I asked for advice about how to be with someone in hospice care: "Remember, it is their story; you are just holding the book."

Become a Compassionate CareGiver - Reduce Stress. Avoid Burnout.

Don't confuse accuracy with the truth. The way the CaredFor tells his story now is his truth. The details may differ, but even in the differences there is a truth being expressed. Your job as the CareGiver is to be able to discern the truth in the differences. What is the CaredFor expressing now?

I'll close this chapter with a story of how I made a memory, not misery.

About a month before my mother died, I decided it would be fun to take mom out to eat one of her favorite foods, hot dogs, or as she like to call them, frankfurters. Now, you know frankfurters have a bad reputation in some circles. Some call them tube steaks made with mystery meat. I doubt a nutritionist would recommend them to someone with an advanced liver disease.

At this stage, I figured how much could one frankfurter hurt her?

The decision to take my mother out to get a frankfurter created a lasting memory for me. I took her to Nathan's Famous in the food court of Pier 17 at the foot of Fulton Slip in lower Manhattan. Pier 17 overlooks the East River. For me, it was about a 20-minute walk from her apartment.

It was a Sunday afternoon when I asked my mother whether she wanted to go to Nathan's to get a frankfurter. She nodded yes.

Having grown up in New York in the 1920s and 1930s, it is likely my mother had had the opportunity to have a frankfurter at the original Nathan's Famous in Coney Island. Nathan Handwerker, a Polish immigrant, started the original five cent hot dog stand on the corner of Surf and Stillwell Avenues in Brooklyn, just a few blocks from the Atlantic Ocean and the beach. My father may even have taken her there while they were dating.

I knew my father was familiar with the area because when we were growing up in the 1950s, he would take my sister and me to the Ravenhall Pool and Baths. Ravenhall had an outdoor salt water pool in sight of the beach at Coney Island. Nathan's Famous was only a short walk away.

As a family, we spent time on the beach at Coney Island. When my mother came with us, she would wade into the ocean until the water got about waist high. Since she hadn't learned to swim, she would stand in the surf as the waves broke around her. Sometimes the waves knocked her down.

So, it was just possible that my father did take my mother to Nathan's Famous for frankfurters, fries, and a Coke long before I was born.

On that cold, partly sunny winter Sunday afternoon, I bundled up my mother. As she got comfortable in her wheel chair, I covered her legs with a blanket. We were now ready to head down to Nathan's Famous at the Pier 17 Mall. This area has a history for both me and my mother.

In high school, before the mall was built, I would go to see the *Peking*, a four-masted barque whose berth was the pier right next to what would become the Pier 17 Mall. That pier berthed several ships that were the prized displays of the South Street Seaport Museum on Fulton Street.

Many times, when I was restless, my mother would say: "Richard, why don't you go down and see your sea gulls?" I would spend hours there watching the sea gulls fly.

The Pier 17 Mall is a little less than a mile from her apartment. It is multi-storied mall. The lower floors have restaurants and shops. One half of the top floor is a food court that overlooks the East River. There is a balcony with reclining chairs and benches.

In pleasant weather, it is a great place to watch sea gulls fly, hover, and dive in search of food. When there are no sea gulls to watch, there are ships, barges, and tugboats working their way up and down the East River to grab your attention.

That Sunday, I said the same thing to my mother. "Let's go see the sea gulls."

As expected, my mother agreed it was good idea to 'go see the sea gulls.'

It was just above freezing outside and partly sunny. When I got her set in her wheel chair, I made sure she had on her wool hat and gloves. I made sure I had mine, too. I fastened her seat belt and off we went.

I wheeled her down a long corridor to the elevator. As we waited for the elevator, I thought to myself. Will the trip be too hard on her? Will she be warm enough? Will she like her frankfurter?

When the elevator came, I put those questions aside. I wheeled her into the elevator. It's tricky opening an elevator door while at the same time pushing someone in a wheelchair into the elevator. Fortunately, by this point, I had had practice with this maneuver.

There are stairs from the foyer of her apartment building to the sidewalk of the courtyard outside the building. There are two sets of stairs: the twelve narrow steps that most people used and the long, wide steps that people with baby carriages, strollers, and wheel chairs used. Even using those wide steps could be jolting to someone in a wheelchair...if you aren't careful.

I took my time wheeling her down the long, wide steps, minimizing the jolts from step to step as best I could. From there to Pier 17, I knew there wouldn't be any more staircases to cause her jolts.

From the level sidewalks inside the apartment court yard, I wheeled her out to Cherry Street. From there, we made it down Cherry Street, a left at Catherine Slip, and then a right onto South Street.

South Street runs alongside the shore of the East River, and underneath the last few miles of the East River Drive. There isn't a side walk on the river side of South Street. Instead there is a paved pathway that the New York City Parks Department built with the intention of having a pathway all around the island of Manhattan. I took advantage of this pathway to get my mother to the Pier 17 Mall.

Just before we reached Pier 17, we passed behind the Fulton Fish Market. I wheeled a little faster through this part of the trip because there is a distinctive aroma from the fish market stalls that is not pleasing to the nose. It was good the Fulton Fish Market was closed; the aroma was not as strong as when it is open.

We had both passed by the Fulton Fish Market either in a car or on foot numerous times before. It was something we were already used to.

Sundays are usually a busy day at Pier 17. Because of the wintry weather, it wasn't as crowded as usual this Sunday afternoon. It is a challenge to navigate someone in wheelchair through a crowded mall.

Most people were taking the escalator to get to the upper floors of the mall. That made it easy for us to find an empty elevator to get up to the food court.

When we arrived at the food court, I wheeled her past the Nathan's counter on our way to find a table with a view. It was too cold to take her out to the balcony. We found a comfortable table. I unbundled her and positioned her wheel chair by the table.

I went back to Nathan's to buy her a frankfurter, fries, and a Coke. I brought her meal back to the table. I watched her eat. I don't think the frankfurter was as good as the original Nathan's, but I think she was satisfied. She didn't really say much about the food.

Of course, she encouraged me to go outside to the balcony so I could get a better view of the sea gulls. There weren't many sea gulls flying about that afternoon but there were a few. After she finished eating, I wheeled her closer to the balcony so she could get a better view, too. Then we began our trip back home.

For me, it was a memorable afternoon. I'm sure mom enjoyed it, too. She got to eat one of her favorite foods, she got some fresh air, cold though it was, and we got to share some time just being together.

There were no pills to give her, no temperature to take, no blood pressure cuff to put on her wrist, just time to be together.

As you progress on your journey of care giving, look for opportunities to make memories, not misery. This will reduce stress in the daily routine of care giving as it gives you something fun to do. At the same time, it provides a break for the CaredFor.

Here are few tips on how to 'make memories, not misery.'

1. Think small, inexpensively. This is not about granting a final wish to the CaredFor. You are not the Make a Wish Foundation.

2. Start by asking the CaredFor what are her favorite things to do. If the CaredFor has memory issues or has trouble communicating, music is a good place to start. Find out what music was popular during early adulthood and play that. I have witnessed people in senior care facilities come to life when the music they are familiar with was playing. In some memory care facilities, music activities are part of the daily program.

3. Consider activities that you would enjoy, too. As they say, 'it takes two to tango.' If you are having fun, it can be contagious. If you aren't, that can be contagious, too.

4. Don't anticipate whether the activity will become a "memory." The proof is in the pudding. Some activities won't work out – it may rain or be too cold the day you decide to go somewhere.

5. Do it anyway. Yes, it may be raining. Yes, it may be cold but find ways to overcome the weather. A memory may spring out of the way you chose to adapt. One day in the future, for example, when dressing for chilly weather, you may see in the closet a coat, a scarf, or a hat that brings back fond memories.

6. Be imaginative. You don't always have to be practical.

7. Be spontaneous. Not every activity has to be planned.

Chapter 11 "When the Music's Over…Turn Out the Lights"

lyrics from "When the Music's Over"
on the album, **Strange Days** by The Doors (1967)

When I got the call from the hospice facility that my mother had died, I quickly dressed and rushed to the hospice facility. I remember running from one street to another, calculating as I ran, where I would be more likely to find a taxi at 2 a.m. on a Sunday morning. After several minutes, I found one.

I gave the taxi driver the address of Beth Israel Hospital, First Avenue and 15th Street. Hospice was on the third floor of the hospital.

My mind was racing. I remember dropping my wallet as I was getting prepared to pay the fare. When I looked down to pick it up, I found a $20 bill between the back seat of the cab and the car door. I felt like I had been given a gift.

When I arrived, I went to the information desk on the hospice floor of the hospital. There was a woman on duty. I gave her the card for the funeral home director. The has made sure the information was already on file. As it turned out, she already had called the funeral home.

On the Thursday before my mother died, the hospice chaplain advised me to have arrangements with a funeral director in place. Otherwise, he told me I would have to claim my mother's body from the county morgue. That's good advice for all CareGivers – have a funeral director in place well before it appears necessary. That's one piece of advice I am glad I followed.

On Friday, I had gone to Vanilla's Funeral home to make the arrangements. The funeral director, Joe Vanilla, was a classmate of mine in grammar school. Back then, it was his father's business. I didn't know Joe had taken over the funeral home. The last time I had seen Joe was at our graduation from grammar school. Dealing with an old friend made arranging the funeral much easier for me.

Now, less than 48 hours later, two men from Vanilla's Funeral Home were at the hospice preparing to take my mother's body from her room.

Looking back, I don't know why I had rushed to the hospital. There really was nothing for me to do that needed immediate attention. I went into her now empty room and collected the few possessions my mother had left.

Since I wasn't in the room before they removed her body, I was concerned I wouldn't find a small book I had left under her pillow. It was miniature sized version of a book from the Zohar[1] that gives comfort to the sick. As I gathered up her possessions, I found the book.

When I left Beth Israel Hospital, it was raining. I was in a daze at that point. I don't remember how I got home. I presume I caught a cab. I don't remember much about the rest of that morning.

I guess you could say all I had left to do when I got home was to go to bed and 'turn out the lights.'

Unfortunately, that's not the case. There is a lot to do after a loved one dies.

Just as with care giving, there are a lot of day-to-day details to handle.

For me, among the things to do, were notifying family of the death; being at the funeral home for each day and evening of the wake; going out to dinner with the family after the wake; attending funeral services; going to the cemetery for the burial; another family dinner after the burial.

In our family, there is a tradition that the wake lasts at least three days. With my mother's wake, it lasted four days. We added an extra day because it snowed one of the scheduled days.

I did appreciate having family and friends around me at the wake at the funeral home. By the time my mother was buried, I had reached a point where I wanted to be alone for a while. I needed time by myself to grieve.

We talked about grieving in chapter 9, "Grief & Loss." As I said before, do give yourself time to grieve. Find your own place to grieve. It's OK to go off by yourself to take a walk or whatever. Don't remain isolated. It's tough to console yourself. Stay engaged.

After the activities related to the funeral are over, the next set of activities to deal with involve settling the affairs of the CaredFor. Depending on which legal arrangements were in place prior to the death of the CaredFor will determine what is necessary to settle affairs. As the CareGiver, you should have become aware of these legal arrangements as soon as possible after assuming the role of CareGiver.

One of the more emotionally difficult tasks is handling the possessions of the CaredFor that remain after all the legally directed distributions. It took me several months to settle my mother's affairs. Though I did it all by myself, I suggest you get the support of a trusted friend or family member to assist with packing up what remains. Otherwise, it may become an emotionally overwhelming process to decide what to dispose of and what to keep.

All these activities are going on while you are dealing, consciously or not, with what to do with rest of your life. At least that's how I was feeling.

As with care giving, there is a tendency to want to *do* something without first considering what you want to *be*. This is golden opportunity. For the first time in your life, you have a chance to step back and ask yourself the hard questions. Who am I? Where am I going? With whom do I want to be? Why am I here?

After the intensity of care giving, I had to ask myself these questions. I had stepped out of the world of information technology for a year. Did I really want to continue to be a missionary for software companies preaching the gospel of technology? Given the value I received from the brief time my mother was in hospice care, I had the desire to work for a hospice company.

When I went online to apply for a hospice job, I found I couldn't meet the requirements for the jobs posted. I didn't have the right letters after my name. I had an MBA from a prestigious business school, but hospice organizations didn't list MBA in the list of qualifications. I saw letters like MSW, Ph.D., M.D. R.N., LPN, CNA. I didn't have those letters after my name, so I gave up on the idea working for a hospice company. Several years later, I become a hospice volunteer. I found it rewarding.

Hospice organizations are always looking for volunteers. Medicare requires that volunteers provide 5% of the work a hospice organization does.

Because I needed to earn a living, I did wind up going back into technology. I couldn't afford to retrain to qualify for a job in health care.

I went to work for a newly formed hardware company. A colleague from a software company I had worked for in the past suggested I join him at this new company. This was the first computer hardware company I had ever worked for.

It didn't last long. I was let go after barely two years. The company closed its doors the following year. Ironically, instability of the software that ran the hardware components was at the heart of why the company went out of business.

As we used to joke in the software industry, "hardware is just an expensive paperweight without good software."

Now I was faced with the question again. What do I want to do now? That was the wrong question to be asking. I really needed to understand who I wanted to become. I needed to ask myself who I wanted to be. Then I could decide what to do.

Dear CareGiver, this is what I recommend highly that you do now. Spend time asking: who do you want to be? What is your highest joy? Seek that.

You'll need guides to help you with these questions. It is a rare individual who can guide herself on the journey of self-discovery.

The guides may be found in people, or books, or workshops. As the proverb goes, "when the student is ready, the teacher will appear." Stay alert! Stay awake!

Be open to what is going on around you. Learn to start looking with the eyes of the heart as well as the eyes of the mind.

Does this sound impractical? Too philosophical? Too spiritual? Too woo-woo? It may. Trust me as one who has been on this journey, this is the most practical advice I can give you.

Yes, the demands of family and finances will beckon. They will demand your attention. Don't give in right away. Carve out time for yourself. Just as when you were a CareGiver, you can't care for another unless you care for yourself...first!

It may sound selfish, even self-indulgent. Overall, to do otherwise is selfish. You won't be any good to family and those around you, if you continue to live the 'unexamined life[2]' you may have been living before.

I end this chapter here, because at this point, there is nothing more I can offer you, dear CareGiver, nothing more I can say to you that will make a difference.

But now it's up to you to give yourself the biggest gift you can...the time TO BE.

[This page is intentionally left blank.]

Wrapping Up

We have looked at ways to shift the paradigm of care giving from doing to being, from fighting death and disease to embracing life and healing. It comes down to finding the unity in how you are *being* as a CareGiver and in what you are *doing* as a CareGiver. It comes down to learning to think non-dualistically. This is a spiritual way of thinking, not a logical way of thinking.

The realm of logical thinking requires opposites or dualism. Right-wrong, black-white, good-bad, hard-soft, etc. You cannot recognize darkness without light. You cannot know silence without sound. You cannot talk about up unless there is a down. The logical mind wants to put things into categories.

So, too, there is dualism in care giving. There are the things to do and there is a way to be.

The compassionate CareGiver learns to bring together the way of being a care giver with doing what a CareGiver does. The compassionate CareGiver recognizes the importance of the way you are being as you do the tasks of care giving. Your attitude is contagious, for better or worse.

The compassionate CareGiver no longer needs to stop to think about his attitude. The attitude of the compassionate CareGiver **is** compassion. It is out of compassion, the compassionate CareGiver does what he does without judgment. He does so without the sense of obligation, guilt, or duty. Thus, the CareGiver becomes free of the conditions that lead to stress and the condition some call CareGiver burnout.

The traditional paradigm of care giving has the CareGiver believe that you continue to give until you have no more to give. The tendency is to put the needs of the CaredFor first. There is the mistaken belief that if the CareGiver doesn't do it, it won't get done.

The realm of care giving is a spiritual journey. On a spiritual journey, it is important to be aware of where you are now. The journey is as important as arriving at the destination. In care giving, the destination is either the death or the healing of the CaredFor. For the compassionate CareGiver, either outcome is acceptable.

The compassionate CareGiver is not attached to a result. The compassionate CareGiver has learned to "let go and let God" while at the same time "praying as though everything depended on God while working as though everything depended on you."

Yes, care giving is a spiritual path. On the spiritual path, we learn to pray first, then to act.

For those who do not believe in God, Allah, Buddha, the Christ, or a transcendent power greater than themselves, consider what those who accept the 12 Step Program of Alcoholics Anonymous do: act as if it were true.

I do not know how one gets through the journey of care giving if you only can rely on yourself. The task of care giving is much larger than the individual.

Regardless of your spiritual posture, the essence of being a CareGiver is to become a compassionate presence for the CaredFor while listening to the CaredFor with a compassionate ear.

With the publication of this book, I have developed a website with a blog about care giving as well as other information about care giving. You can find it at http://caregiverja.com. *I look forward to meeting you there.*

Epilogue

Death & Dying

As I lay her down to sleep,
I feel like crying
As there is no denying
The suffering that she feels.

What is death to the dying?
A hoped for relief?
Or just a thief
Blindly stealing her thread of life?

What is death to the living
Who watch the dying live?
A reminder to forgive
Anything that may remain,
That unforgiven, will cause pain.

Is death a healing or a cure?
Does it bring peace?
Or is it just a release
To the next stage on the path?
(Assuming you believe in an
aftermath.)

How do the living bring
Healing to the dying?
Do we sing?
Do we plant a seed?
Do we recite a creed,
Praying that faith yields belief

That leads to hope,
So that neither the living nor
The dying will feel the grief
Of a life cut short, incomplete?

Words on a page,
Even in this scientific age
Do play a part in the interaction
Among death, the dying, and the living.

For when I can no longer think
Of things to say
As I watch her will receding
Before the onslaught of pain,
I can read from a book
professionally written
And share the wisdom of one who
Has been there before as more
Than an observer at death's door.

As I struggle to know what else to do or say,
To ease her on her way,
Words I read teach me
That what's left for me to do is to:

Be hopeful.
Be thankful.
Be truthful.
Be still.
Be.

Richard Anastasi
A New York City Apartment
February 7, 2004

[This page is intentionally left blank.]

Acknowledgments

Don't you just hate having to read through the acknowledgment section of a book? The author thanks people who usually you don't know. The author has forgotten to thank the people who should have been thanked, and you are wondering why you should bother reading this section of the book. What's in it for you?

Frankly, nothing -- unless you know me or my family and are wondering whether you are mentioned here.

I would ask you to keep reading, though, out of respect for the people I have acknowledged. You never know. One day, without knowing it, you may have made a difference in the life an author and wind up in the acknowledgments.

There are two sets of people I want to acknowledge: those who supported me while I was caring for my mother and those who have supported me while I was writing this book.

I want to thank Pat Finnell for the times she came to the hospital to help me with tasks I couldn't do for my mother, for inviting me out to dinner or to a movie, and for helping me find Café Lika.

Café Lika was a restaurant/bar on Orchard St on the Lower East Side of Manhattan that became my respite center.

I want to thank the staff of Café Lika who were on duty while I was a CareGiver: David, Amit, Orit, Amanda, and of course Lika, the owner of Café Lika and its sister restaurant, Simone's. I also want to thank 'the regular' customers at these restaurants who enriched my life during this tough time. I don't remember your names, but I remember many of you. These were places I went where I could get away from the stress of being a CareGiver. Unfortunately for me, both restaurants closed after my care giving days in New York City.

I found a similar place in Dallas during the writing of this book, Chocolate Secrets on Oak Lawn Avenue in Dallas. In addition to having great chocolate, ice cream, wine, coffee, and live music, it's a great atmosphere to relax and write. I want to express my thanks to the staff, from A to Z, [AJ, Buddy, Carmen, Carolyn, Chris, Dawn, Jake, Libby, Petra, Riley, Stevie, Tony, Tracie, Tray, Zeb] and to some of the musicians who performed there (Riley, Terry, Jason, Darwin, Kimberly Nicole) while I was writing and editing this. You always made me feel welcome.

Of course, none of this would have been possible had Pam Eudaric-Amiri not decided to start Chocolate Secrets over 10 years ago. Thanks Pam for your love and support.

I want to express my appreciation for my friends in Talk of the Tower Toastmasters Club who heard many speeches based on the content of the book and for my friends in Toastmasters District 50.

The support of the men in a Friday morning group (which continues to meet at Farina's Winery & Café in Grapevine, TX) kept me going when I needed it most. Thanks, Gary, Malcolm, Tony, Steve, Louie, David S., David G., Rollie, Russ, all the Mike's, Justin, Walt, to name a few.

My health advisors, staff, and friends at Erb Family Wellness have helped keep me physically and mentally sound (though some may question this). Thanks Dr. David and Kimberly Erb and Dr. Dee. I must not fail to thank Dr. Becky and Dorota who introduced me to Maximized Living Doctors and Erb Family Wellness.

My spiritual communities at the Church of the Incarnation and St. Albert the Great Priory in Irving, TX as well as my Centering Prayer Groups have been sources of strength and support for longer than the time it has taken to write this book.

Though she was not directly involved in the care giving or the writing of this book, special thanks to Carol Smith who provided unsolicited and much appreciated financial support and friendship during the research and writing phases for this book.

Thanks to Dilly & EO. You know why.

I am sure there is someone I should have acknowledged but didn't. If you are that someone, please forgive for me.

Peace & Joy,
Richard

Notes

Prologue: And I Closed the Book
[1] The book set: **Kitchen Table Wisdom** & **My Grandfather's Blessings** by Rachel Naomi Remen, M.D., (New York: Riverhead Books, 2000)

[2] Definition of primary biliary cirrhosis: see citation at **https://www.nlm.nih.gov/medlineplus/ency/article/000282.htm** "Primary biliary cirrhosis is irritation and swelling (inflammation) of the bile ducts of the liver. This blocks the flow of bile, which damages the livers cells and leads to scarring called cirrhosis...The cause of inflamed bile ducts in the liver is not known. However, primary biliary cirrhosis is an autoimmune disorder. That means your body's immune system mistakenly attacks healthy tissue. "
Courtesy of Medline Plus, a service of the U.S. National Library of Medicine at the National Institute of Health.

Introduction
[1] Gail Sheehy, **Passages in Caregiving – Turning Chaos into Confidence**, (New York: William Morrow, an Imprint of HarperCollinsPublishers, 2010), pages 53, 313.

[2] Rachel Naomi Remen, M.D., **Kitchen Table Wisdom, Stories That Heal** (New York: Riverhead Books, 1996)

[3] Rachel Naomi Remen, M.D., **My Grandfather's Blessings, Stories of Strength, Refuge, and Belonging**, (New York: Riverhead Books, 2000)

Chapter 1: And Lead Us Not Into [the] Temptation...of Doing
[1] Joel Arthur Barker, **Paradigms, The Business of Discovering the Future**, (New York: Harper Collins, 1992)

[2] Katherine Dowling Singh, **The Grace in Aging** (Boston: Wisdom Publications, 2014)

[3] Edward W. Bastian and Tine L. Staley, **Living Fully Dying Well, Reflecting on Death to Find Your Life's Meaning** (Boulder, CO: Sounds True, 2009)

[4] Dr. Charles Majors, Dr. Ben Lerner with Sayer Ji, **The Cancer Killers – The Cause Is The Cure** (Orlando, FL: Maximized Living™, 2013)

Chapter 2: It's in How You Approach the Task: The Origin of the P Dance

[1] Eckhart Tolle, **The Power of Now, A Guide to Spiritual Enlightenment,** (Novato, CA: New World Library, 1999)

Chapter 3: Becoming a Compassionate Presence

[1] Pema Chödrön, **Good Medicine,** *How to Turn Pain Into Compassion with Tonglen Meditation,* (insert of CD set, Pema Chödrön, © 2001 Sounds True, Inc. Boulder, CO 80306)

[2] *ibid.,* page 2.

[3] *ibid.,* page 3.

[4] *ibid.,* page 5.

[5] Pema Chödrön, **When Things Fall Apart: Heart Advice for Difficult Times**, (Boston: Shambhala Publications, Inc., 2007)

Chapter 4: "But I Gotta Do Something"…Yes, Listen

[1] Marshall B. Rosenberg, **Nonviolent Communication, A Language of Life**, (Encinitas, CA: Puddle Dancer Press, 2005)

[2] Rev. Lucy Sanders, health care chaplain, Sherrill House nursing facility, Jamaica Plain, Mass. quoted in radio interview show "**Humankind**," show #169, "Chaplains," www.humanmedia.org

Chapter 5: Starting with the End in Mind

[1] "Gloria T. Anderson, **The African-American Spiritual and Ethical Guide to End-of-Life Care**, http://www.hearttones.com and http://eolcareguide.org

² **The Conversation Project,** http://theconversationproject.org/
³ For more information about the body's 7-year cycles, go to: http://dreamhawk.com/body-and-mind/every-seven-years-you-change

⁴ Kathleen Dowling Singh, **The Grace in Aging – Awaken as You Grow Older (**Wisdom Publications, Boston, 2014) Page 3, 45-57.

⁵ Thich Nhat Hanh, **No Death, No Fear, Comforting Wisdom for Life,** (New York: Riverhead Books, 2002)

⁶ Thomas Keating, **Open Mind, Open Heart – The Contemplative Dimension of the Gospel** (Element Inc., Rockport, Massachusetts, 1986) page 109.

⁷ Thomas Keating, **Invitation to Love – The Way of Christian Contemplation** (Continuum, New York, 2002) page 6, page 145: "Emotional Programs for Happiness – the growth of the instinctual needs of survival/security, affection/esteem, and power/control into centers of motivation, around which our thoughts, feelings, and behavior gravitate."

Chapter 6: The Healing Power of Place

¹ Esther M. Sternberg, M.D., **Healing Spaces, The Science of Place and Well-Being,** (The Belknap Press of Harvard University Press: Cambridge, Massachusetts, 2009), page 1.

² *ibid.* page 3.

³ Krista Tippett with Esther Sternberg, **On Being**, radio program http://www.onbeing.org/program/the-science-of-healing-places/4856/audio?embed=1

⁴ Atul Gawande, **Being Mortal, Medicine and What Matters in the End**, (New York, Metropolitan Books, Henry Holt and Company, 2014) pages 100ff, 115ff, 129ff.

⁵ Paul Markowitz, **Senior Living Specialists,** http://www.SeniorLivingSpecialists.com

Chapter 7: Stop Fixin' the Disease – Heal the Person

[1] The World Health Organization defines health as: "Health is a state of complete physical, mental and social well-being and not merely the absence of disease or infirmity."
http://www.who.int/about/definition/en/print.html

[2] You can learn more about the Five Essentials at
http://maxliving.com/five-essentials

[3] You can learn more about Essential #5, Minimize Toxins at
http://maxliving.com/five-essentials/minimize-toxins/

Chapter 8: Pain & Suffering

[1] Therese Schroeder-Sheker,
https://en.wikipedia.org/wiki/Therese_Schroeder-Sheker

[2] Therese Schroeder-Sheker: Music & the Art of Dying,
http://www.youtube.com/watch?v=gppfjwu4xXk, interview hosted by Thinking Allowed, www.thinking-allowed.com

[3] **What is Music-Thanatology?**, http://www.mtai.org/index.php/what_is

[4] Dr. Richard Fratianne, **Music to reduce pain for Burn Patients**, Dr. Richard Fratianne, director emeritus of MetroHealth Medical Center's burn unit in Cleveland, OH believes music therapy reduces pain. He has conducted several studies over the last decade. Fratianne hopes someday music therapy is covered by insurance, just as physical therapy and occupational therapy are now.

Dr. Richard Fratianne benefits from music therapy firsthand, January 31, 2011.
http://www.cleveland.com/healthfit/index.ssf/2011/01/dr_richard_fratianne_benefits.html

Evelyn Theiss, **The Plain Dealer,** MetroHealth Medical Center studies show music therapy reduces pain (video):

http://www.cleveland.com/healthfit/index.ssf/2011/01/music_therapy_eases_patients_p.html

Chapter 9: Grief & Loss

[1] Elizabeth Kübler –Ross, **On Death and Dying – What the dying have to teach doctors, nurses, clergy, and their own families**, (New York: Scribner, 1969)

[2] David Kessler's website explaining the 5 stages of grief:
http://grief.com/the-five-stages/

Chapter 10: Make Memories, Not Misery

[1] Richard Rohr, **Immortal Diamond, The Search for Our True Self**, (San Francisco, CA: Jossey-Bass, A Wiley Imprint, 2013)

Chapter 11: "When the Music's Over...Turn Out the Lights"

[1] The Zohar is the literature of Jewish mystical tradition known as Kabbalah.

[2] "The unexamined life is not worth living." This quote is attributed to Socrates. It appears in Plato's **Apology**, which is a recollection the speech Socrates delivered at his trial. See a discussion of this quote at:
http://www.consciousearth.us/socrates-unexamined-life.html

Resources

Introduction

Armstrong, Karen, **Twelve Steps to a Compassionate Life** by Karen, New York: Anchor Books, a Division of Random House, Inc., 2015

Dyer, Dr. Wayne W., **The Power of Intention – Learning to Co-Create Your World Your Way,** New York: Hay House, 2004

Frenette, David, **The Path of Centering Prayer – Deepening Your Experience of God,** Boulder CO: Sounds True, 2012

Keating, Thomas, **Open Mind, Open Heart – The Contemplative Dimension of the Gospel,** Rockport, Massachusetts: Element Inc., 1986

Remen, Rachel Naomi, M.D., **Kitchen Table Wisdom, Stories That Heal**, New York: Riverhead Books, 1996

Remen, Rachel Naomi, M.D., **My Grandfather's Blessings, Stories of Strength, Refuge, and Belonging**, New York: Riverhead Books, 2000

Ross, Elisabeth Kübler, M.D. **On Death and Dying – What the dying have to teach doctors, nurses, clergy, and their own families,** New York: Scribner, 1969

Chapter 1: And Lead Us Not Into [the] Temptation...of Doing

Barker, Joel Arthur, **Paradigms, The Business of Discovering the Future,** (New York: Harper Collins, 1992)

Majors, Dr. Charles, Lerner, Dr. Ben, with Ji, Sayer, **The Cancer Killers – The Cause is the Cure,** Orlando, FL: Maximized Living™, 2013

Murray, Anne Firth, **Paradigm Found, Leading and Managing for Positive Change**, Novato, CA: New World Library, 2006

Nuland, Sherwin B., **How We Live,** New York: Vintage Books, A Division of Random House, Inc., 1997

Rosenberg, Marshall B., Ph.D., **Nonviolent Communication – A Language of Life,** 2nd Edition, Encinitas, CA: Puddle Dancer Press, 2005

Singh, Kathleen Dowling, **The Grace in Aging – Awaken as You Grow Older,** Boston: Wisdom Publications, 2014

Chapter 2: It's in How You Approach the Task: The Origin of the P Dance

Bastian, Edward W., Ph.D. and **Staley,** Tina L., L.C.S.W., **Living Fully Dying Well – Reflecting on Death to Find Your Life's Meaning,** Boulder, CO: Sounds True, 2009

Sheehy, Gail, **Passages in Caregiving – Turning Chaos into Confidence,** New York: William Morrow, An Imprint of HarperCollinsPublishers, 2010

Tolle, Eckhart, **The Power of Now, A Guide to Spiritual Enlightenment,** Novato, CA: New World Library, 1999

Chapter 3: Becoming a Compassionate Presence

Armstrong, Karen, **Twelve Steps to a Compassionate Life** by Karen, New York: Anchor Books, a Division of Random

Chödrön, Pema **Good Medicine,** *How to Turn Pain Into Compassion with Tonglen Meditation,* (insert of CD set of Pema Chödrön), Boulder, CO: Sounds True, Inc., 2001

Chödrön, Pema, **When Things Fall Apart: Heart Advice for Difficult Times,** Boston: Shambhala Publications, Inc., 2007

Chapter 4: "But I Gotta Do Something" ...Yes, Listen

Albom, Mitch, **Tuesdays with Morrie – An Old, a Young Man, and Life's Greatest Lesson,** New York: Doubleday, a division of Random House, 1997

Rosenberg, Marshall B., Ph.D., **Nonviolent Communication – A Language of Life,** 2nd Edition, Encinitas, CA: Puddle Dancer Press, 2005

Chapter 5: Starting with the End in Mind

Anderson, Gloria T. **The African-American Spiritual and Ethical Guide to End-of-Life Care,** http://www.hearttones.com and http://eolcareguide.org

Attwood, Janet Bray, Attwood, Chris, with Dvorak, Sylvia, Ph.D., **Your Hidden Riches – Unleashing the Power of Ritual to Create a Life of Meaning and Purpose,** New York: Harmony Books, 2014

Crisp, Tony, **Every Seven Years You Change,** http://dreamhawk.com/body-and-mind/every-seven-years-you-change/

Hanh, Thich Nhat, **No Death, No Fear, Comforting Wisdom for Life,** New York: Riverhead Books, 2002

The Conversation Project http://theconversationproject.org/ The Conversation Project is dedicated to helping people talk about their wishes for end-of-life care.

Chapter 6: The Healing Power of Place

Cason, Ann, **Circles of Care – How to Set Up Quality Home Care for Our Elders,** Boston: Shambhala Press, Boston, 2001

Gawande, Atul, **Being Mortal, Medicine and What Matters in the End,** New York: Metropolitan Books, Henry Holt and Company, 2014

Markowitz, Paul, founder and President, **Senior Living Specialists,** (214) 929-5055, serving Dallas-Ft Worth, TX, www.SeniorLivingSpecialists.com

Sternberg, Esther M, M.D., **Healing Spaces, The Science of Place and Well-Being,** Cambridge, Massachusetts: The Belknap Press of Harvard University Press, 2009

Chapter 7: Stop Fixin' the Disease – Heal the Person

Hawkins, David R., Ph.D., **Power vs. Force –The Hidden Determinants of Human Behavior,** New York: Hay House, Inc., 1995

"The teachings of Devotional Nonduality emphasize the core truths of the world's greatest spiritual traditions: kindness and compassion to everything and everyone (including oneself), humility, forgiveness, simplicity, lovingness as a way of being, reverence for all of life, devotion to Truth, and surrender to God. It is a direct path to Enlightenment in which each internal progression of love and integrity uplifts the whole of existence: 'We change the world not by what we say or do but as a consequence of what we have become.'"

Chapter 8: Pain & Suffering

Hollis, Jennifer L., **Music at the end of life. Easing the Pain and Preparing the Passage**, Santa Barbara, CA: Praeger, an imprint of ABC-CLIO, LLC, 2010.

This book highlights the unique role music has come to play in hospice and palliative medicine. Jennifer Hollis interweaves narrative memoir, the personal experiences of fellow music-thanatologists and caregivers, and extensive research to demonstrate the transformative power of music when curing is no longer an option. Through story after unforgettable story, Hollis offers a new vision of end-of-life care, in which music creates a beautiful space for the work of letting go, grieving, and saying goodbye.
http://www.abc-clio.com/ABC-CLIOCorporate/product.aspx?pc=D3744C

Mizes, Carol Shively, **Music therapy eases patients' pain, helps on road to recovery** - January 31, 2011
http://www.cleveland.com/healthfit/index.ssf/2011/01/music_therapy_eases_patients_p.html

Carol Shively Mizes is a certified music therapist on staff at MetroHealth Medical Center

What is Music-Thanatology? http://www.mtai.org/index.php/what_is

Chapter 9: Grief & Loss

Attig, Thomas, **How We Grieve, Relearning the World**, New York: Oxford University Press: 1996

Collins, Judy, **The Seven T's, Finding Hope & Healing in the Wake of Tragedy**, New York: Jeremy P. Tarcher/Penguin, 2007

Kessler, David, Ross, Elisabeth Kübler, M.D., **On Grief & Grieving, Finding the meaning of grief through the five stages of loss**, New York: Scribner, a division of Simon &Schuster, Inc., 2005

Ross, Elisabeth Kübler, M.D. **On Death and Dying – What the dying have to teach doctors, nurses, clergy, and their own families**, New York: Scribner, 1969

Chapter 10: Make Memories, Not Misery

Chittister, Joan, **Welcome to the Wisdom of the World**, Grand Rapids, Ml.: William B. Eerdmans Publishing, 2007

Rohr, Richard, **Immortal Diamond, The Search for Our True Self,** San Francisco, CA: Jossey-Bass, A Wiley Imprint, 2013

Chapter 11: "When the Music's Over...Turn Out the Lights"

Attwood, Janet Bray, Attwood, Chris, with Dvorak, Sylvia, Ph.D., **Your Hidden Riches – Unleashing the Power of Ritual to Create a Life of Meaning and Purpose**, New York: Harmony Books, 2014

Check for updates to these resources as well as additional content at my blog site at: http://caregiverja.com

Bibliography

Albom, Mitch, **Tuesdays with Morrie – An Old, a Young Man, and Life's Greatest Lesson,** New York: Doubleday, a division of Random House, 1997

Armstrong, Karen, **Twelve Steps to a Compassionate Life** by Karen, New York: Anchor Books, a Division of Random House, Inc., 2015

Attig, Thomas, **How We Grieve, Relearning the World**, New York: Oxford University Press: 1996

Attwood, Janet Bray, Attwood, Chris, with Dvorak, Sylvia, Ph.D., **Your Hidden Riches – Unleashing the Power of Ritual to Create a Life of Meaning and Purpose,** New York: Harmony Books, 2014

Barker, Joel Arthur, **Paradigms, The Business of Discovering the Future,** (New York: Harper Collins, 1992)

Bastian, Edward W., Ph.D. and Staley, Tina L., L.C.S.W., **Living Fully Dying Well – Reflecting on Death to Find Your Life's Meaning**, Boulder, CO: Sounds True, 2009

Cason, Ann, **Circles of Care – How to Set Up Quality Home Care for Our Elders,** Boston: Shambhala Press, Boston, 2001

Chittister, Joan, **Welcome to the Wisdom of the World**, Grand Rapids, Ml.: William B. Eerdmans Publishing, 2007

Collins, Judy, **The Seven T's, Finding Hope & Healing in the Wake of Tragedy**, New York: Jeremy P. Tarcher/Penguin, 2007

Dyer, Dr. Wayne W., **The Power of Intention – Learning to Co-Create Your World Your Way,** New York: Hay House, 2004

Frenette, David, **The Path of Centering Prayer – Deepening Your Experience of God,** Boulder CO: Sounds True, 2012

Gawande, Atul, **Being Mortal, Medicine and What Matters in the End**, New York: Metropolitan Books, Henry Holt and Company, 2014

Hanh, Thich Nhat, **No Death, No Fear, Comforting Wisdom for Life,** New York: Riverhead Books, 2002

Hawkins, David R., Ph.D., **Power vs. Force –The Hidden Determinants of Human Behavior**, New York: Hay House, Inc., 1995
Hollis, Jennifer L., **Music at the end of life. Easing the Pain and Preparing the Passage**, Santa Barbara, CA: Praeger, an imprint of ABC-CLIO, LLC, 2010.

Keating, Thomas, **Open Mind, Open Heart – The Contemplative Dimension of the Gospel,** Rockport, Massachusetts: Element Inc., 1986

Keating, Thomas, **Invitation to Love – The Way of Christian Contemplation,** New York, Continuum, 2002

Kessler, David, Ross, Elisabeth Kübler, M.D., **On Grief & Grieving, Finding the meaning of grief through the five stages of loss**, New York: Scribner, a division of Simon & Schuster, Inc., 2005

Majors, Dr. Charles, Lerner, Dr. Ben, with Ji, Sayer, **The Cancer Killers – The Cause is the Cure,** Orlando, FL: Maximized Living™, 2013

Murray, Anne Firth, **Paradigm Found, Leading and Managing for Positive Change**, Novato, CA: New World Library, 2006

Nuland, Sherwin B., **How We Live,** New York: Vintage Books, A Division of Random House, Inc., 1997

Rohr, Richard, Immortal **Diamond, The Search for Our True Self,** San Francisco, CA: Jossey-Bass, A Wiley Imprint, 2013

Remen, Rachel Naomi, M.D., **Kitchen Table Wisdom, Stories That Heal**, New York: Riverhead Books, 1996

Remen, Rachel Naomi, M.D., **My Grandfather's Blessings, Stories of Strength, Refuge, and Belonging**, New York: Riverhead Books, 2000

Rosenberg, Marshall B., Ph.D., **Nonviolent Communication – A Language of Life,** 2nd Edition, Encinitas, CA: Puddle Dancer Press, 2005

Ross, Elisabeth Kübler, M.D. **On Death and Dying – What the dying have to teach doctors, nurses, clergy, and their own families**, New York: Scribner, 1969

Sheehy, Gail, **Passages in Caregiving – Turning Chaos into Confidence**, New York: William Morrow, An Imprint of HarperCollinsPublishers, 2010

Singh**,** Kathleen Dowling, **The Grace in Aging – Awaken as You Grow Older,** Boston: Wisdom Publications, 2014

Sternberg, Esther M, M.D., **Healing Spaces, The Science of Place and Well-Being,** Cambridge, Massachusetts: The Belknap Press of Harvard University Press, 2009

Tolle, Eckhart, **The Power of Now, A Guide to Spiritual Enlightenment,** Novato, CA: New World Library, 1999

www.ingramcontent.com/pod-product-compliance
Lightning Source LLC
Chambersburg PA
CBHW070053120426
42742CB00048B/2511